3 0132 01430 5739

D0495016

QUICK AND EASY
Patchwork
and Appliqué

QUICK AND EASY
Patchwork
and Appliqué

EDITED BY

ROSEMARY WILKINSON

NORTHUMBERLAND COUNTY LIBRARY	
30132014305739	
Bertrams	
746.445	£14.99

NEW
HOLLAND

First published in 2006 by
New Holland Publishers (UK) Ltd
London I Cape Town I Sydney I Auckland
www.newhollandpublishers.com

Garfield House, 86-88 Edgware Road, London W2 2EA

80 McKenzie Street, Cape Town 8001, South Africa

Unit 4, 14 Aquatic Drive, Frenchs Forest, NSW 2086, Australia

218 Lake Road, Northcote, Auckland, New Zealand

2 4 6 8 10 9 7 5 3 1

Text, photography and illustrations © 2006 New Holland Publishers (UK) Ltd
Quilt designs copyright © Jane Coombes, Nikki Foley, Janet Goddard,
Liz Lynch, Carol O'Riordan, Mary O'Riordan, Gail Smith, Sarah Wellfair,
Alison Wood, Dorothy Wood

Copyright © 2006 New Holland Publishers (UK) Ltd

All rights reserved. No part of this publication may be reproduced, stored in
a retrieval system, or transmitted in any form or by any means, electronic,
mechanical, photocopying, recording or otherwise, without the prior written
permission of the publishers and copyright holders.

ISBN 1 84537 425 8

Editor: Rosemary Wilkinson
Design: Frances de Rees
Photographs: Shona Wood
Illustrations: Carrie Hill
Template diagrams: Stephen Dew

Reproduction by Pica Digital PTE Ltd, Singapore
Printed and bound in Malaysia by
Times Offset (M) Sdn Bhd

NOTE
The measurements for each project are given in imperial and metric. Use only
one set of measurements – do not interchange them because they are not
direct equivalents.

CONTENTS

Getting Started

Types of fabric to use for patchwork and appliqué

The most popular type of fabric for patchwork and the easiest to work with is 100% cotton. Fabric designers produce co-ordinating ranges of patterns specifically for patchwork, using a common colour palette, so that all the designs will work together. These fabrics are of a very good quality and can be purchased from specialist patchwork and quilting shops. If you are going to spend time and money making a quilt, it's nice to know that you are working with good quality materials, so that the quilt will last for a long time.

Cotton is also very suitable for hand-stitched appliqué, as it can be folded and manipulated and a crisp edge can be obtained, even when working with quite small pieces. It's also suitable for bonded appliqué.

Manufacturers have recently started to introduce different fabrics, such as silk and damask, co-ordinating with their ranges for us to experiment with, which is an exciting development.

Some fabrics, such as polycottons, are really too "bouncy" to enable the quilter to achieve a crisp finish when the fabrics are folded and stitched. As you become more experienced, you will become aware of how different fabrics perform.

A good rule to follow for a professional finish is to make sure that all the fabrics in the quilt are the same weight and thickness. However, there are exceptions to the rule, such as crazy patchwork, a traditional Victorian technique, and in modern quilting, art quilts also break the rules, where paper, plastic and other unusual fabrics could be used.

One other important factor to consider when buying fabric is the size and direction of the pattern. Bold designs can sometimes be too big for small patches, although this can work to advantage if the pieces are cut carefully. Some fabrics have a very obvious one-way design, which can cause a problem when cutting small pieces; however, they can be very effective when used in borders.

Fabric preparation

Many quilters prefer to wash all their fabrics before use and there are two reasons for this. Firstly, cotton shrinks when washed, so it's better to sort this out before piecing. Secondly, washing dark fabrics helps get rid of any excess dye.

Equipment
General

Anyone with a basic sewing kit at home could take up patchwork by hand. However if you wish to piece your quilt by machine, there are some basic tools you will need to invest in. Designed for speed and accuracy, they go hand-in-hand with your sewing machine and will enhance your sewing. Sewing machines vary from those offering a basic straight stitch to those with a wide range of decorative stitches. The choice largely depends on your price range, although a machine with a swing needle for zigzag stitching is a requirement for appliqué work.

The three most essential tools are a rotary cutter, a self-healing mat printed with measurements and an acrylic ruler. These all come in different sizes, but as a basic guide, a 45 mm cutter, a medium size board and a ruler long enough to span the board should get you started (diagram 1).

1 Rotary cutter. The cutter is capable of cutting through several layers of fabric at a time and for this reason is extremely sharp. It will have a guard to cover the blade when not in use.

Please train yourself to put the guard on at all times, when you are not actually using it. Also keep in a safe place away from children and animals.

Avoid rolling over a pin or other solid

diagram 1

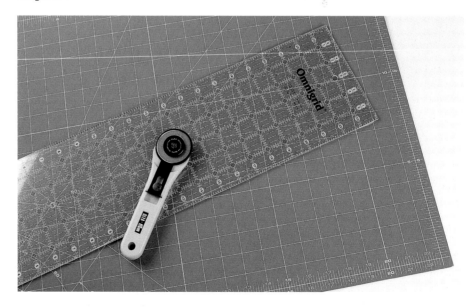

object as this will ruin the blade by giving it a dull spot. If you have not used a cutter before, try practising on old sheets before using new fabric. Eventually you will have to replace the blade, through normal wear and tear. Keep the cover from the new blade and use it to dispose of the old one safely.

2 Self healing mat (or board). Usually green or grey in colour, these are available with either metric or imperial measurements. After you make a cut with the rotary cutter the board closes up again, so that it can be used repeatedly. They come in a range of sizes. The biggest ones make cutting strips easiest but a smaller size, such as A3, is more portable.

Note
Keep the board flat and away from sources of heat, such as radiators, as once warped it will be useless.

3 Ruler. Eventually you will probably buy several different rulers, as they are available in different sizes each suitable for different jobs. A square ruler can be useful when working with blocks, and they also come in different sizes. Every ruler should have accurate measurements marked on it, and also may have guidelines to help you cut angles of 45 and 60 degrees.

Other items you will need:
Template plastic: available from quilting shops. Cardboard can be used instead but is not so durable.
Pins: flower headed pins are best, as they lie flat, but can be expensive.
Pencils: with sharp points, (disposable propelling pencils are good), also marking pencils in silver or yellow (for dark fabrics).
Scissors: I would recommend a dressmaking size and a craft size; a smaller embroidery size pair could be very useful

for smaller work. You will also need scissors which can be kept just for paper. Paper will blunt your fabric scissors and these need to be kept nice and sharp.
Needles: a selection of sizes is useful, plus "quilting/betweens" for hand quilting. Buy size 8 or 9 to start with and progress to 10s if you get really good at hand quilting. The higher the number, the smaller the needle.
Sewing machine needles: refer to your sewing machine manuals for information on which needle they suggest and always keep a spare packet with your machine. Specialist needles are available, such as for machine quilting (finer) and for metallic thread (large eye with a groove in the side of the needle).
Safety pins: you can buy special quilters' safety pins which are slightly curved on the bottom to enable you to pin the three layers of the quilt together. If you have to move the quilt about, they stay in place better than normal pins, which tend to wriggle their way out.

For hand quilting you will need:
Thimbles, or finger protection: these are used to protect the fingers during hand quilting, which involves pushing the needle through the layers of fabric, wadding and backing to form tiny running stitches. In one quilt there will be thousands of these stitches and you would find that without protection, the skin of your quilting fingers above and below the quilt would quickly become sore. For this reason there are various types of thimbles and finger protectors on the market. It is a matter of personal choice (and a certain amount of trial and error) as to which combination of these you can work with.
Quilting hoop: If you are going to be doing a lot of quilting, you may wish to buy a quilting hoop. These are either wooden or plastic and range in size from 4 in/10 cm upwards. Bind the hoops with white cotton tape to prevent them damaging the fabric of the quilt.

For appliqué you might find these useful:
Freezer paper: for making templates.
Small appliqué pins: tiny pins which help hold the appliqué pieces in place until they are stitched down.
A pin board: on to which you can pin small pieces, which helps to keep everything in place until needed.

Rotary cutting
Practise on old sheets or unwanted fabric and don't try to cut through too many layers at first. Remove any clutter from your workspace and have all your equipment within easy reach. Make sure the work table is at a comfortable height.

1 Take your fabric to the cutting board, fold it in half wrong sides together with selvages aligned at the top and the cut edge facing towards your cutting hand. Ideally, the board should be big enough to fit the depth of the folded fabric. Before cutting any pieces, you need to ensure that the cut edge of the fabric is straight, i.e. at right angles to the selvages, as accuracy depends on this. It will also help you to establish a straight grain of fabric. This is the line of the threads making up the fabric weave. Place the ruler on the fabric close to the cut edge, aligning one of the horizontal lines on the ruler with the fold of the fabric. If the cut edge is not exactly parallel to one of the vertical lines on the ruler, cut off a small strip to straighten (diagram 2).

diagram 2

2 Turn the straight edge to face in the opposite direction. Now you will be using the ruler as a tool to cut accurate pieces. Cutting instructions in a quilt pattern usually start with asking you to cut a strip, then to turn the strip and cut off small pieces, either squares or rectangles. For example, you may need to end up with multiple 4 in/10 cm squares. To do this, first cut a 4 in/10 cm strip off your fabric, as follows. Lay the fabric on the mat, with the straight edge of the fabric to the left (or right if you are left-handed). Line up the 4 in/10 cm linear marking of the ruler against the edge of your fabric. The area now trapped under the ruler will be a 4 in/10 cm strip. Double check this by counting on your ruler from right to left. Now press down firmly on the ruler with your left (or non-cutting) hand, take the rotary cutter in the other, line the blade up against the ruler just below the fabric and, pushing away from you, cut along the length of the ruler going from bottom to top (diagram 3). Congratulations - you have now mastered the rotary cutter!

diagram 3

3 Turn the strip of fabric, so that it is lying sideways across the board and trim off the selvages. You can now cut this in the same way to form a 4 in/10 cm square. Remember to work from the left, trap the required amount of fabric under the ruler (by lining up with the 4 in/10 cm line on the ruler), check and when happy, cut from bottom to top. This automatically produces two squares (as the fabric

is folded). Repeat this until you have the required amount of squares (diagram 4). This is known as cross-cutting.

diagram 4

The cutting instructions in the designs which follow will specify that the strips should be cut to a specified depth across the width of the fabric, then cross-cut into specified pieces. They assume the rotary cutting method described above will be used.

You can cut strips, rectangles and triangles by this method, you just need to be organised and be able to count!

Chain piecing

If you have identical pairs of shapes to be sewn together, you can save time and thread by taking them to the machine and stitching continuously across the pieces until all the pieces are sewn together (diagram 5). You can then cut the thread between the pairs and press the individual pieces – often referred to as "units". This can be used for triangles, squares and rectangles.

diagram 5

Quick pieced triangles

There are many more tried and tested methods to speed up your patchwork.

One which is very successful if you are making lots of squares made up of two triangles (called "half-square triangles") also works particularly well with the chain piecing method.

Someone has worked out the maths for this, but basically, if you want to end up with a particular sized square, you will need to add on $3/8$ in/1.75 cm to the finished size to obtain the cut size. For instance, if you want two half-square triangles to end up as a $4 \frac{1}{2}$ in square, you must cut the original squares $3/8$ inch bigger, that is $4 \frac{7}{8}$ in. Or in metric, a finished 11 cm square would need to be cut to 12.75 cm. If you use this calculation every time you want to make half-square triangles by the following method, then you can't go wrong.

1 Take two different squares of the required size and colour to the cutting board. Place them right sides together, with the lighter one uppermost. Taking a ruler and sharp pointed pencil, draw a diagonal line across the square from corner to corner, repeating as many times as necessary on the remaining pairs of squares (diagram 6).

diagram 6

2 Machine stitch ¼ in/0.75 cm to the left of the diagonal line on the first pair of squares, then chain-piece all the remaining squares in this way. When complete, turn the chain round and start stitching from the other end ¼ in/0.75 cm away from the opposite side of the diagonal line in the same way (diagram 7).

diagram 7

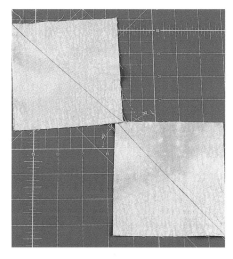

3 Cut the pieces apart. Take one set of squares to the cutting board and cut across the marked diagonal line. Open out, press and you will have two squares made up of two triangles (diagram 8). Repeat for all the squares.

diagram 8

Appliqué

We have talked about piecing, now some information about appliqué, which is the application of pieces of fabric to a background fabric. There are quite a few ways by which we can successfully apply one fabric to another, creating a pattern or even a new surface.

Needle turn appliqué

This type of appliqué is hand-stitched and there are a few different ways of doing it. The freezer paper method, which is an easy one to start with, is described first.

Freezer paper method

Freezer paper is marketed in the USA as a paper to wrap frozen goods at home; however it has been used in appliqué for some time and can be obtained from specialist patchwork quilting suppliers. It is shiny on one side and matt on the other. The shiny side can be ironed down on to the fabric, lifted and repositioned, time after time. Alternatively it can be left in place as a former for the appliqué shape, as in this method.

If you cannot obtain freezer paper you can do this with ordinary printer paper but it will not have the advantage of sticking to the fabric.

1 Choose a simple shape, such as a heart, and don't start too small. Place a piece of freezer paper, shiny side down, over the shape, and trace on to the matt side (diagram 9).

diagram 9

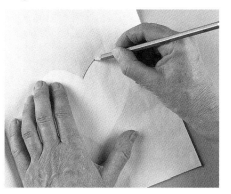

2 Cut out the freezer paper shape exactly on the marked line to make a template and iron down on to the wrong side of the fabric, which should be at least ¼ in/0.75 cm bigger all the way round than the shape. Trim the seam allowance to a scant ¼ in/0.75 cm (diagram 10).

diagram 10

3 Leaving the freezer paper in place, pin the shape to the background fabric using appliqué pins. Thread a needle with thread to match the appliqué shape, bring the needle to the front of the fabric, then use the tip to turn under ¼ in/0.75 cm of the appliqué fabric. You will be able to feel the freezer paper inside, and you can use it as an edge against which you can turn the fabric, creating a crisp fold. Take a tiny appliqué stitch (like a slip stitch) on the fold of the material, from the front to the back of the work to stitch down this turning (diagram 11).

diagram 11

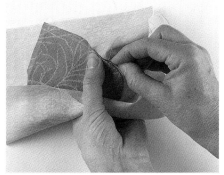

Continue in the same way round the heart shape and stop about 1 in/2.5 cm from the beginning. Take the freezer paper out and stitch up the gap.

Paper template

Another method is to make a paper template of the desired shape and draw round it on the right side of the fabric.

1 Cut out the fabric ¹/₄ in/0.75 cm outside the marked line, then place the fabric shape over the paper template, fold over the seam allowance and loosely tack in place (diagram 12).

diagram 12

2 Pin this piece to the background fabric and stitch using a tiny appliqué stitch as before (diagram 13). The paper can either be left in place permanently or can be removed through a tiny incision from the reverse side in the background fabric.

diagram 13

Interfacing

A third method is to cut out your shape in the chosen fabric including a ¹/₄ in/0.75 cm seam allowance, then cut a piece of interfacing roughly the same size. Place the interfacing on the right side of the fabric and stitch the two together taking a ¹/₄ in/0.75 cm seam allowance, leaving a small gap to turn the shape inside out (diagram 14). Trim the interfacing back to the fabric shape.

diagram 14

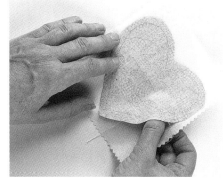

You will find that you have a neat edge which you can the apply to the background in the normal way, with the added advantage that you do not have to needle turn (diagram 15).

diagram 15

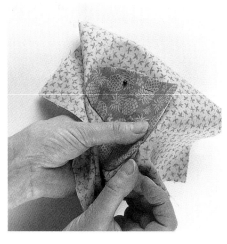

If you are working with sharp curves and intricate shapes you may find it necessary to nick the seam allowance slightly, to allow the fabric to "give" more.

Bonded appliqué

In this relatively modern method, the pieces are applied to the background fabric using fusible webbing. This is usually finished off with machine stitching round the raw edge (satin stitch, open zig-zag or blanket stitch), but can also be done by hand (normally blanket stitch). Fusible webbing is very thin fabric glue, attached to a sheet of transparent paper. Initially it will be rough on one side (the glue side) and smooth on the other. (You can trace on to this side.)

1 Make a template of a shape, such as a heart, that you wish to appliqué to your fabric. Trace the heart on to the smooth side of the fusible webbing. Cut out roughly outside the marked line (diagram 16).

diagram 16

2 Place the fabric for the appliqué wrong side up on the work surface and put the fusible webbing shape, rough side down, on top. Iron to fix in place. Now cut the shape out exactly on the marked line (diagram 17).

diagram 17

3 Peel off the paper backing, leaving the glue on the fabric. Position the shape where you want it, glue side down, on the right side of the background fabric and carefully iron it to bond the two fabrics together (diagram 18). This will now stay in place until it is stitched.

diagram 18

4 Stitch in place with a satin or zigzag stitch. The ideal is to just cover the edge of the shape, without stitching too much into the background fabric. This takes practice (diagram 19).

diagram 19

You can cut out some very tiny intricate shapes with this method, but remember that by tracing on to the backing paper your shape will be **reversed** when you finally iron it in place. If you want a true image i.e. the same way round, you must trace the image on tracing paper, reverse it and trace again on to the fusible web.

Hints and tips for appliqué stitching by machine

These hints and tips also apply to blanket stitch or open ziq- zaq if used in this way.

● I always recommend that you practise first if you have not done machine appliqué before. First set your machine to a satin stitch and do a sample.

● Every machine varies slightly, so it is important that you make a note of any stitch settings (width and length) that you find work well. (You should be able to vary the density of the cover of the satin stitch by altering the stitch length and width.) If, for instance, you practise on calico, you can write the information on the sample of calico.

● You may also find it useful to make a note of thread type, needle size, etc. If you file these, you will build up a good portfolio of samples for later reference.

● It is a good idea to start with the needle down in the fabric, then you know exactly where you are starting. If the appliqué shape has a gentle curve, you should be able to manoeuvre the needle around the shape as you stitch.

● If you are working with geometric or particularly fiddly shapes you will need to stop at each sharp corner, preferably with the needle down in the work, lift up the presser foot, turn the fabric, put down the presser foot and start stitching again.

● Also plan your work so that you change the thread colour as little as possible. On a project this could mean doing all the blue first, then the red, and so on.

Raw edge appliqué

Mainly used in modern quilts, this type of appliqué can be done with or without fusible webbing, but if done without, pins or tacking should be used to anchor the fabric while it is being stitched.

1 Taking the heart shape again, cut it out in fabric to the exact size you want (do not add a seam allowance), then pin, tack or fabric glue in place.

2 To anchor the shape to the background, you can use a variety of threads and stitches, which may be decorative or functional, hand or machine (diagram 20). With time this kind of work will probably fray a little, but in modern quilts this is acceptable.

diagram 20

Other surface decorations
Couching

Particularly useful for adding surface decoration to your quilt, couching refers to the laying down of threads or thin strips of fabric on to the surface, then stitching down by hand or machine – usually also with decorative stitches. Any stitch on the machine which involves the needle swinging from side to side can be used.

Waddings

To be a quilt your work must officially have three layers: a top (which may be pieced), backing fabric and wadding sandwiched in between.

The three most popular types of wadding are 100% polyester; this comes by weight, either 2 oz or 4 oz, and also special ones for quilting, 100% cotton and a mix of 80% cotton and 20% polyester. Normally they are white or cream in colour. Black or dark grey polyester wadding is available too; if you are making a black or very dark quilt, it would be advisable to use this.

Within these categories there are many variations on offer and by the time you have made two or three quilts, you will find a favourite. Also available, but expensive and not widely stocked, are silk and wool wadding. Silk drapes beautifully and wool re-creates the quilts of old because it shrinks when washed, giving a wrinkled appearance to the quilt. Cotton wadding also shrinks, some are pre-washed, and all usually come with some information about this, so check when you buy. One more type of wadding worth mentioning is thermal, which is useful for making table mats and similar items. It lies very flat, so can be useful for other items too. You may consider using fleece (the type fleece jackets are made of) on the back of a quilt, as in "Promenade Throw" on page 64, which doesn't need a wadding, but I would not recommend this for a large project.

You may hear of "loft" mentioned in reference to wadding. This is the thickness of the wadding which will affect the depth of the quilted effect.

Another term you may come across is "bearding". This is the amount of little fibres of the wadding which come through the fabric when you are quilting. This is the reason you may wish to use black wadding for darker projects.

Your choice of wadding may also be affected by the person who will be using the quilt. For babies natural fibres are recommended, but if you're making a playmat or picnic mat which would need constant washing, you would probably choose polyester. Quilts are not recommended at all for babies under six months.

Wadding comes in various widths, and shops will probably stock rolls of a certain width, you may have to order it especially if the quilt is unusually large. It also comes in pre-cut pieces suitable for different beds from cot to king size.

Waddings suitable for appliqué

Before deciding which wadding to use for appliquéd projects, you should decide what type of quilting you are going to use. For hand quilting, you should choose one of the softer types of wadding that will be easier on your hands; this means probably one of the polyester ones, or very thin cotton if it is soft.

Waddings left to right: silk, cotton, 2 oz cream polyester, black cotton, 80%/20% cotton/polyester, wool, grey and white polyester

For machine quilting, you have a much wider choice, as it is the machine that is going to be doing the hard work for you.

Take advice from the instructions on the side of the pack of wadding as to how close together the quilting lines should be, whether 4, 6, or 8 in/10, 15 or 20 cm. Normally appliquéd projects will have outline quilting around the appliqué shapes, so may be quite densely quilted in some cases. If in doubt, I would always recommend that you try making a sample, with a small quilt sandwich.

Quilting
Making up the quilt sandwich
As mentioned earlier, a quilt must have three layers. In order to achieve a good finish, you must put the layers together carefully, keeping them as flat as possible before quilting can commence.

Ideally you should buy the backing and wadding so that they are slightly larger – say 3 in/8 cm all round – than the quilt top. Keep it this way until all the quilting is finished.

1 Tape the quilt backing right sides down to a large table or to the floor.

2 Centralise the wadding on top of this.

3 Finally add your quilt top right way up (having ironed it first).

4 Pin the layers together – keeping them as flat as possible. Start pinning your quilt from the centre outwards (diagram 21).

diagram 21

5 Tacking can now start. Take some tacking thread and a large needle, and, always working from the centre outwards, tack through all three layers in a grid of lines approximately 4 to 6 in /10 to 15 cm apart (diagram 22). I cannot stress how important this is if you want to achieve good results for your quilting. It is just not worth cutting corners, even if it seems a little tedious, it will be well worth it in the end.

diagram 22

The "sandwich" is now ready to be quilted. Hopefully you will enjoy this bit. Your quilt top will come to life once it is quilted. Again we have to make choices as to the method of quilting. Some people will enjoy hand quilting more than machine quilting and vice versa, and some people do both.

Transferring designs

One frequently asked question is how to transfer a quilting design on to your quilt or indeed what type of quilting to use.

The transfer of the design on to the quilt should always be done before layering. Stencils are available, as are special pens which are air or water dissolvable, and yellow and silver pencils (for dark fabrics) sometimes come with an eraser, or just wear off in time, ordinary thin lead pencils can also be used.

Another method is to draw the design on to tissue paper, to tack this to the quilt, stitch over it and then tear it away afterwards.

For the design there are many choices. Basically, a geometric quilt will call for geometric style quilting, and an abstract quilt might call for more abstract, random quilting. Unless you want to break all the rules! You can do all of the above things with machine quilting. Machine quilting will appear as a continuous line of stitching on the surface of the quilt, unlike hand quilting which is a broken line. However some modern machines have a facility which makes the stitching look like a broken line.

If you are a beginner then I would definitely recommend the free machine quilting method to start with.

Machine quilting

For this you will need a walking foot. Consult your sewing machine supplier about this (have make and model number handy), so that you get the right one. If you want to do "free" machine quilting, you will also need a darning or embroidery foot, and be able to drop the feed dogs of your machine – more about that later. The object of the walking foot is to feed the layers of the quilt evenly over the feed dogs of your machine as you quilt. If you were to use an ordinary foot, it would apply too much pressure to the backing fabric, giving you major problems (and puckers) in your quilt.

Always start quilting in the centre of the quilt. If it is a large quilt you will probably need to roll it up in order to do this. Try not to let the weight of the quilt drag on the needle as this will affect the quality of the stitching. Practice makes perfect, and it is probably best if you start with a small project and work up.

Whatever type of quilting you decide to do, there will always be thread ends to deal with. These should be sewn securely in to the middle layer of the quilt, so that they cannot ever come unravelled. Try "easy threading" needles if you only have very short ends of thread left. These have a slot in the top of the needle and can be very useful.

Quilting in-the-ditch

This is a method of machine quilting, which is not always visible. It is stitched along a seam line, by slightly parting where the seam lies, then letting it settle back after stitching (diagram 23). The loft of the wadding helps to disguise the quilting. Sometimes people use invisible thread for this method.

diagram 23

Echo quilting

This is a term used to describe quilting a $^1/_4$ in/0.75 cm away from the shape or seam line (diagram 24).

diagram 24

Free machine quilting

This is also described as "taking the needle for a walk" – you will see why when you give it a try. As mentioned above you will need a darning or embroidery foot and to drop the feed dogs on the sewing machine for this type of quilting (refer to manufacturer's handbook if in doubt).

The most popular type of free machine quilting is "vermicelli" which is a meandering stitch where the paths of the stitching do not cross (diagram 25). The beauty of this is that it can be done large or small and you can cover large open spaces on quilts with it. For different stitches, you can experiment, and basically, if you can draw it with a pencil – try doodling in a continuous line without taking the pencil off the paper – then you can quilt it.

diagram 25

Other types of pattern include loops, spirals, feathers, flowers, butterflies, shells, and many more.

Hand quilting

It takes a lot of practice to become good at hand quilting but this is necessary if you are contemplating doing a lot of it.

You will need a quilting hoop and thimbles (see page 7). The design needs to be marked on the work before placing in the hoop (see page 13). Unlike for a piece of embroidery, the work needs to be slack in the hoop. Hand quilting needles are tiny (see page 7). The stitches look like a running stitch on the surface but are done in such a way that the back is identical to the front. Make sure you are sitting comfortably before you start, and that you have good light. Always start in the centre of the quilt and work outwards.

1 Thread your needle with one of the good quality hand quilting threads available. (They are usually waxed to aid quilting.) Knot the end. From the back of the work (underneath the fabric contained in the hoop) come up through the layers of the quilt sandwich with the needle. The knot can be hidden among the layers, by "popping" it through the back layer. Do this by applying gentle force.

2 Now the needle should be on the uppermost side of the work. You should be able to see your pattern clearly. Push the needle and thread straight down until you feel the receiving finger, which should be ready underneath, place your thumb slightly ahead of the first stitch to act as a tension guide (diagram 26).

diagram 26

3 Now guide the needle back up to the surface, by almost bouncing off the underneath thimble. Repeat this, eventually achieving several stitches at once. This has sometimes been described as a "rocking" action. At first this will seem difficult to achieve, but if you practise regularly you will be able to load the needle with a number of stitches.
Note: Take the quilt out of the hoop in between working sessions, so that it doesn't mark the fabric.

Big stitch quilting

A modern version of the traditional hand quilting, this has evolved along with art quilts and contemporary work, where there is a crossover between embroidery and quilting. Threads such as pearl cotton can be used to great effect to both quilt and embellish at the same time. As the name suggests, the stitches are larger than normal, but still fairly even in size (diagram 27). A chenille needle would be helpful for this as it is sharp with a big eye, for thick threads to pass through Other stitches, such as cross stitch, herringbone and feather stitch, could also be done in this way.

diagram 27

Binding the quilt

Once the quilting is finished, remove all tacking, then you will need to bind the edges of your quilt. This can be done in a fabric of your choice but it is quite often darker than the other fabrics as this acts to frame the quilt.

Continuous method

To work out how much binding you need, measure the outside edge of your quilt all the way round and add 3 – 4 in/ 8 – 10 cm. Patchwork fabric is normally 44 in/112 cm wide, so divide the measurement by 44 if working in inches or 112 for centimetres, to obtain the number of strips you need to cut across the width of the fabric to achieve the total required. If, for example, this is five, multiply by the depth of the strips i.e. 2½ in/6.5 cm, to find the amount of fabric needed, which in this case will be 12½ in/32.5 cm. Join these strips together to form a continuous strip.

When binding a quilt using the continuous strip method, it is best to cut it 2½ in/6.5 cm wide and fold it in half as you stitch it on to the quilt. Do this as follows, using the walking foot.

1 Put the edge of your quilt under the foot of the machine, lay the folded strip of binding on top of the quilt so that the raw edges line up. Taking a ¼ in/0.75 cm seam allowance, start stitching the binding on to the right side of the quilt (diagram 28).

diagram 28

2 When you reach a corner, you should mitre your binding to achieve a good finish. To do this, remove the quilt from the machine and place on a flat surface, with the binding just stitched at the top edge. Fold the binding up and away from the quilt to "twelve o'clock", creating a 45° fold at the corner. Fold the binding back down to "six o'clock" aligning the raw edges of the binding to the raw edge of the quilt. The fold created on the binding at the top should be the same distance away from the seam as the width of the finished binding (diagram 29).

diagram 29

3 When this stage is complete, turn the binding to the back and hand stitch it in place using a matching thread along the stitching line just made.

Using four separate pieces

1 Measure each edge of the quilt. Cut the binding as in the above method but keep it in four pieces. If the quilt is large, you may need to join strips to get the appropriate lengths.

2 Measure the quilt through the centre from top to bottom. Cut two of the binding pieces to this length. Pin and stitch these to two sides of the quilt, easing to fit. Fold the binding to the back and stitch in place.

3 Measure the centre of the quilt from side to side, then add ½ in/1.5 cm to this measurement. Cut two of the binding pieces to this length. Neaten the short ends by turning in ¼ in/0.75 cm at each end, then pin and stitch to the top and bottom of the quilt as before (diagram 30).

diagram 30

Hanging sleeve

If your quilt or wallhanging is going to be hung, whether at an exhibition or at home, you will need a hanging sleeve. With a little thought a sleeve can be added at the binding stage, with fabric saved from the backing of the quilt.

1 Cut the fabric 10 in/25 cm deep x width of quilt. Neaten the short ends with a small hem, as these will be on show.

2 Fold it in half lengthways and line it up with the top back edge of the quilt before binding. When the binding is stitched in place, it will attach the raw edge of the sleeve (diagram 31).

diagram 31

3 It only remains for you to hand stitch the folded edge into position on the back.

If you want a temporary sleeve, I would recommend a piece of fabric hand stitched on after completion of the quilt.

Labelling

Always add a fabric label to your quilt to record details such as your name and date and the title of the piece.

Daisy Chain

DESIGNED BY

Alison Wood

Daisies scattered on the green grass give a summer freshness to this bed topper or throw, which would look good when used in the garden or conservatory. The finished blocks are large at 12 in/30 cm square, and the appliqué shapes simple, so the quilt goes together quickly for maximum impact with relatively little effort.

MATERIALS

All fabrics used in the quilt top are 45 in/115 cm wide, 100% cotton

Daisy petals, centres and chain blocks: yellow, ¾ yd/0.70 m; white, 2 yds/1.75 m

Background, borders and binding: green, 4½ yds/4 m

Fusible webbing: 3 yds/3 m, 18 in/45 cm wide

Backing: 4½ yds/4 m or one piece, 80 in/190 cm square

Wadding: cotton or 80:20 cotton/polyester mix for machine quilting; cotton/cotton blend or 2 oz polyester for hand quilting, 72 x 92 in/183 x 234 cm

CUTTING

1 From the yellow fabric, cut two strips, 2½ in/6.5 cm deep, across the width, and three strips, 4½ in/11.5 cm deep. Cross-cut each of the 4½ in/11.5 cm strips into nine 4½ in/11.5 cm squares, making 27 yellow squares.

2 From the white fabric, cut two strips 2½ in/6.5 cm deep, across the width and three strips, 4½ in/11.5 cm deep. Cross-cut each of the 4½ in/11.5 cm strips into nine 4½ in/ 11.5 cm squares, making 27 white squares.

3 From the green fabric, cut six strips, 4½ in/11.5 cm deep, across the width and cross-cut into nine 4½ in/11.5 cm squares, making 54 green squares. Cut four strips, 12½ in/31.5 cm deep, across the width and cross-cut into three 12½ in/31.5 cm squares, making 12 large background squares.

4 From the remaining green fabric, cut four strips, 6½ in/17 cm wide, down the length of the fabric for the borders; cut five strips, 2½ in/6.5 cm wide, down the length for the binding.

Quilt plan

Finished size: 72 x 72 in/183 x 183 cm

5 For the 12 daisy appliqué blocks, enlarge the daisy petal template on page 20, then trace 12 daisy petal shapes and 12 daisy centre shapes on to the smooth side of the fusible web. Cut out, leaving a ¼ in/0.75 cm allowance outside the marked lines. Press the fusible web daisy centres on to the wrong side of the remaining yellow fabric and the fusible web petal shapes on to the wrong side of the remaining white fabric. Cut out following accurately the marked lines on the fusible web papers.

STITCHING

To make the daisy blocks:

1 Remove the paper from the back of one of the white daisy petal shapes and place it, right side up, in the centre of the right side of one of the green 12½ in/31.5 cm squares.

2 Peel the paper from the back of one of the yellow daisy centres and place it, right side up, in the centre of the white daisy petal shape. Press in place. Repeat with the remaining 11 daisy blocks.

3 Stitch a small decorative zig-zag, using white thread, around the daisy petal shapes as close as possible to the edge. Do the same with the yellow centres using yellow thread. Repeat for all the daisy appliqué blocks.

To make the 13 chain blocks:

4 For each chain block, one central four-patch block is required. Stitch one white 2½ in/ 6.5 cm strip and one yellow 2½ in/6.5 cm strip, right sides together and taking a ¼ in/0.75 cm seam allowance, along the length of the strips. Repeat with the other pair of white and yellow 2½ in/6.5 cm strips. Press the seams towards the yellow fabric.

NOTE

Careful attention to pressing at this stage will give accurate blocks. Press the seams joining the strips flat first i.e. with the strips still right sides together; this "sets" the seam, causing the thread to sink into the fabric a little which helps to give a flatter, crisper finish. Then, use the side of the iron and flip the top strip open, pressing from the right side to ensure there are no little pleats beside the seams. Try to press, rather than to iron the fabric as you do not want to curve the stitched strips.

5 Place one pair of stitched strips on top of another pair, alternating the yellow and white fabrics. Align the seam allowances along the length of the strips, they should butt together. Cross-cut the strips into 13 units, each 2½ in/6.5 cm wide (diagram 1).

diagram 1

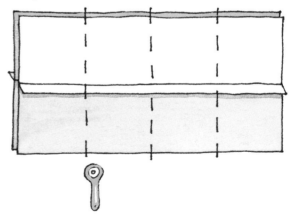

TEMPLATES

daisy petals 50% actual size
- enlarge on a photocopier
by 200%

daisy centre
full size

6 Stitch each unit down one long side with the top seam facing towards the needle: this helps the seam allowances to butt together and gives a well-matched point in the centre of the four-patch block. Make 13 four-patch blocks. Press the seams towards the yellow fabric and see the note on page 21 for reducing bulk in the centre of the block (diagram 2).

diagram 2

NOTE

To reduce the bulk in the centre of a block and to make quilting much easier, try this "trick" with seam allowances. It is very easy to do provided your stitch length is not too short. Hold a four-patch block, wrong side facing, and with the horizontal seam pointing at an angle away from you, gently pull the section of seam allowance on the right-hand side of the patch towards you with your right thumb and index finger, while keeping the left-hand seam allowance pushed away from you. A few stitches in the seam allowance should "pop" open, allowing the seams to lie in opposite directions (diagram 2). Press. I am grateful to Harriet Hargrave, inspirational American quiltmaker and teacher, for showing me the trick with the seam allowance

7 Pin and stitch the yellow, green and white 4½ in/11.5 cm squares together taking the usual seam allowance to make 26 units of three squares each. Press the seam allowances towards the green squares.

8 Pin and stitch one green 4½ in/11.5 cm square on either side of a central four-patch block (diagram 3), taking the usual seam allowances. Make a total of 13 units. Press the seam allowances towards the green squares.

9 Pin and stitch one of the units made in step 7 on either side of the unit made in step 8, reversing the direction at top and bottom, so that the yellow and the white squares form diagonal patterns to make the chain block. Make a total of 13 chain blocks in this way. Press the seam allowances towards the outside of the blocks (diagram 3).

diagram 3

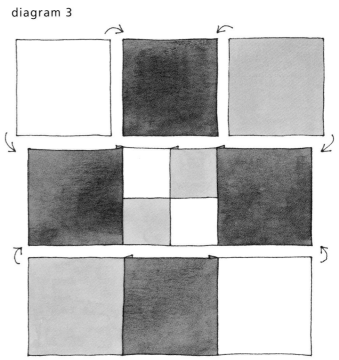

10 Following the quilt plan on page 18, assemble the blocks in five rows of five blocks alternating the chain blocks with the daisy appliqué blocks, ensuring the yellow and white chains connect across the diagonals. Pin and stitch the blocks into rows, taking the usual seam allowances, and press the seams towards the daisy blocks.

11 Stitch the five rows together; start the odd-numbered rows with a chain block, the even-numbered rows with a daisy block. Carefully match seams, and when stitching try to ensure underneath seam allowances are stitched in flat. When all the rows have been joined, press all seams in one direction.

ADDING THE BORDERS

1 Measure the pieced top through the centre from top to bottom. Trim two of the border strips to this measurement. Pin and stitch to the sides of the pieced top. Press the seams towards the borders.

2 Measure the pieced top through the centre from side to side, then trim the remaining two border strips to this measurement. Pin and stitch to the top and bottom. Press as before.

FINISHING

1 Spread the backing right side down on a flat surface, then smooth out the wadding and the patchwork top, right side up, on top. Fasten together with safety pins or baste in a grid.

2 Machine quilt first along the diagonals of the yellow and white chains to criss-cross the quilt. Use thread to match the colour of the chain. Stitch parallel lines either side of the chain blocks, using green thread. Extend the quilting out into the borders. Finally quilt with yellow thread around the daisy centres to secure the middle of each block.

3 Join the binding strips with diagonal seams to make a continuous length to fit all round the quilt and use to bind the edges with a double-fold binding, mitred at the corners.

Alternative colour schemes

1 Pink petals on a soft lavender background for a pretty pastel quilt. 2 Liberty florals sparkle against white: make each daisy different to showcase a collection of small prints. 3 Funky prints on a dark background for a lively version of the design. 4 Yellow daisies with dark centres show that country colours can work just as well as brights or pastels.

Bright Stars

DESIGNED BY

Sarah Wellfair

This simple but effective design gains its impact from the mixing up of stars and squares in four colours, so that no two squares have the same colour combination. It makes a lively throw to brighten up your sofa or could be used as a topper on a child's bed.

MATERIALS

All fabrics used in the quilt top and backing are 45 in/115 cm wide, 100% cotton

Blocks and stars: purple, green, pink, yellow, 19 in/50 cm each

Borders: light purple, 24 in/60 cm

Binding: green, 19 in/50 cm

Fusible webbing: 39 in/100 cm

Backing: bright pink, 60 in/150 cm

Wadding: lightweight, 60 in/150 cm

CUTTING

1 From each of the four block and star fabrics, cut one strip, $10\frac{1}{2}$ in/26.5 cm deep, across the width. Cross-cut the strip to make three $10\frac{1}{2}$ in/26.5 cm squares of each colour; make 12 squares in total.

2 From the light purple fabric, cut five strips, 5 in/12.5 cm deep, across the width, for the borders.

3 From the green fabric, cut four strips, 3 in/7.5 cm deep, across the width, for the binding.

4 Use the template on page 28 to trace 12 stars onto the smooth side of fusible web leaving a $\frac{1}{4}$ in/0.75 cm allowance all around each star. Cut out the shapes just outside the marked lines. Press three star shapes onto the wrong side of each of the remaining purple, green, pink and yellow fabrics. Cut out the stars accurately along the marked lines.

Quilt plan

Finished size: 50 x 40 in/125 x 99 cm

STITCHING

1 Following the quilt plan on page 18, position one star in the centre of each of the purple, green, pink and yellow squares, each star should go on each of three different coloured fabrics, so that no two colour combinations are the same. Remove the papers from the back of the star shapes and press to bond them in place.

2 Stitch a large close zig-zag in black thread all around the edge of each star. When turning a corner, drop the needle over the edge into the background fabric, lift the presser foot and pivot the fabric on the needle until it's in the correct position to stitch the next edge.

3 Arrange the squares in rows of three different colours as desired (see quilt plan), and stitch, right sides together, taking a $1/4$ in/0.75 cm seam allowance (diagram 1). Then stitch the four rows, right sides together, taking a $1/4$ in/0.75 cm seam allowance. Press the seams towards the darker fabrics.

diagram 1

ADDING THE BORDERS

1 Measure the pieced top through the centre from side to side, then trim two of the light purple border strips to this measurement. Pin and stitch to the top and bottom of the quilt.

2 Measure the pieced top through the centre from top to bottom, then cut trim the remaining two border strips to this measurement. Pin and stitch to the sides.

FINISHING

1 Trim the backing and wadding to 2 in/5 cm larger than the pieced top on all sides. Spread the backing right side down on a flat surface, then smooth out the wadding and the pieced top, right side up, on top. Fasten together with safety pins or baste in a grid.

2 Machine quilt in a vermicelli design around the stars using invisible thread and a jeans needle. Leave the borders free.

3 Stitch the binding strips with diagonal seams to make a continuous length to fit all around the quilt, and use to bind the edges with a double-fold binding, mitred at the corners.

TEMPLATE
full size

Alternative colour schemes

1 A dark check with pale blue stars makes a good masculine colourway. 2 Teddy bears and gold stars are perfect for toddlers. 3 Red and beige give a more homespun look. 4 Black and white produce a striking, graphic colourway.

Leaf Wallhanging

DESIGNED BY

Gail Smith

This wallhanging is inspired by the leafy countryside near my home and the vibrant colours of autumn. It will brighten your home even on the dullest winter's day. The embellished panels add a textured finish, and the quilt features different types of leaves stitched by machine appliqué, machine embroidery, raw edge appliqué or machine quilting.

MATERIALS

All fabrics used in the quilt top are 45 in/115 cm wide, 100% cotton

Background fabric: cream print, 1 yd/1 m

Background blocks: mustard yellow, 14 in/35 cm

Embellished panels: multi-coloured pink/orange/yellow, 15 in/35 cm

Sashing and panels: marbled orange, 11 in/27 cm; cranberry, 4 in/10 cm

Batik panels and binding: pink/orange, 21 in/55 cm

Appliqué leaves: lime green, 10 in/25 cm; light green, 4 in/10 cm; bronze effect, 4 in/10 cm; tan, 5 in/12 cm

Fusible webbing: $1\frac{1}{2}$ yds/1.5 m

Backing and hanging sleeve: one piece, 40 x 48 in/105 x 122 cm and one piece, $4\frac{1}{2}$ x $37\frac{1}{2}$ in/11.5 x 95.5 cm

Wadding: lightweight, 40 x 48 in/ 102 x 122 cm

CUTTING

1 From the cream fabric, cut five blocks (see quilt plan on page 32). Plan the cutting carefully to fit the fabric:
$10\frac{1}{2}$ x $11\frac{1}{2}$ in/27 x 29.5 cm (block 1);
$13\frac{1}{4}$ x $26\frac{1}{4}$ in/33.5 x 66.5 cm (block 2);
$9\frac{1}{2}$ x $16\frac{1}{2}$ in/24.5 x 42 cm (block 5);
$12\frac{1}{2}$ x $11\frac{1}{2}$ in/32 x 29.5 cm (block 6);
$12\frac{1}{2}$ x $19\frac{1}{2}$ in/32 x 48 cm (block 7).
Label each block for reference.

2 From the mustard yellow fabric, cut two blocks (see quilt plan):
$13\frac{1}{2}$ x $12\frac{1}{2}$ in/34.5 x 32 cm (block 3);
$10\frac{1}{2}$ x $10\frac{1}{2}$ in/27.5 x 27.5 cm (block 4).
Label each block.

3 From the multi-coloured fabric, cut and label three pieces for the embellished panels (see quilt plan):
$3\frac{1}{4}$ x $11\frac{1}{2}$ in/8.5 x 29.5 cm (piece 1a - attaches to block 1);
$13\frac{1}{4}$ x 6 in/33.5 x 15.5 cm (piece 2a – attaches to block 2);
$12\frac{1}{2}$ x 11 in/32 x 28 cm (piece 6a – attaches to block 6).

Quilt plan

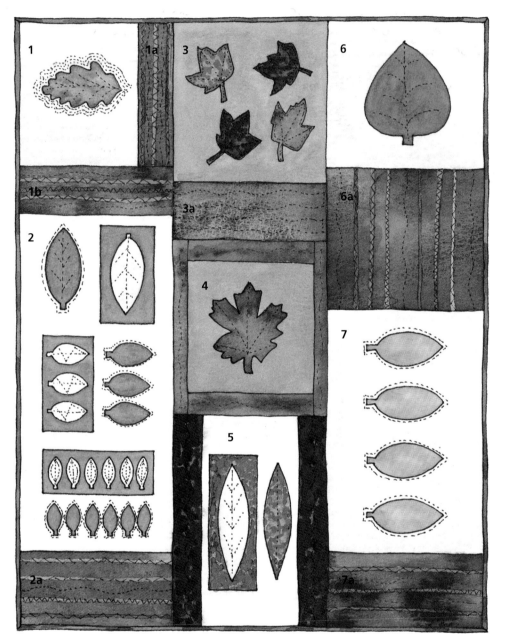

Finished size: 39 x 47 in/97 x 117 cm

4 From the marbled-orange fabric, cut two pieces for the embellished panels (see quilt plan):

13¼ x 4 in/33.5 x 10 cm (piece 1b – attaches to block 1);

12½ x 6¼ in/32 x 16 cm (piece 7a – attaches to block 7);

and cut four strips, 2 x 13½ in/5 x 34.5 cm, for sashing (around block 4).

5 From the cranberry fabric, cut two pieces 2½ x 16½ in/6.5 x 42 cm for sashing (attaches to block 5).

6 From the batik fabric, cut one piece 13½ x 5¼ in/34.5 x 13 cm (piece 3a); cut four strips, 1½ in/4 cm deep, across the width, for the binding. Label all pieces for reference.

7 Use the template patterns on pages 34 to 36 to trace the appliqué leaf shapes onto the smooth side of fusible web, taking care to reverse the shapes where necessary (see quilt plan). Cut out just outside the marked lines. Press the fusible web shapes to the wrong side of the appropriate pieces of fabric. Cut out the shapes following accurately the marked lines on the fusible web papers.

NOTE

Some of the leaf shapes enclosed in a box are both positive and negative, cut from the same piece of fabric. Try to cut them out as accurately as possible. To make it easier to start cutting, fold the fabric in half and make a small cut at the fold using pointed-end scissors (diagram 1). Open out and continue cutting round the shape.

diagram 1

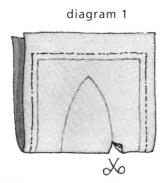

STITCHING

1 Remove the papers from the back of the leaf shapes and position right sides up on each background block as shown in the quilt plan opposite. Press the shapes into place.

2 Use matching threads and stitch around each leaf shape as follows, but do not add leaf veins at this stage:
blocks 1 and 7: blanket stitch; blocks 2, 4 and 5: satin stitch; blocks 3 and 6: edge stitch close to the edge using straight stitch.

3 Decorate and embellish the multi-coloured panels (pieces 1a, 2a, 6a) with machine embroidery, using thick wool or thread; couch them down in rows onto the fabric (diagram 2). Repeat with the two marbled-orange panels (pieces 1b and 7a). Piece 3a between blocks 3 and 4 will be blank at this stage.

diagram 2

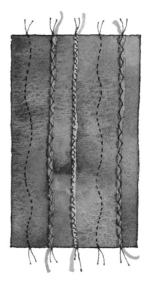

4 Pin and stitch a marbled-orange sashing strip, right sides together, and taking a ¼ in/ 0.75 cm seam allowance, to each of the four sides of block 4, trimming as necessary. Pin and stitch the cranberry sashing strips to the long sides of block 5, right sides together and taking the same seam allowance. Press all seams towards the darker fabrics.

5 Pin and stitch block 1, the oak leaf, to its side panel (piece 1a), right sides together taking the usual seam allowance. Attach piece 1b, right sides together, taking the same seam allowance, and work down the layout to stitch three columns, following the numerical order of the blocks (see quilt plan).

6 Pin and stitch the three columns, right sides together, taking the usual seam allowance. Press seams towards the darker fabrics.

FINISHING

1 Spread the backing right side down on a flat surface, then smooth out the wadding and the pieced top, right side up, on top. Fasten together with safety pins or baste in a grid.

2 Use a walking foot and straight stitch to add quilted veins to the leaves (see dotted lines on templates). Add extra stitching in between the rows of embellishments on pieces 1a, 2a and 6a, and wavy lines in the panel (piece 3a) between blocks 3 and 4. Quilt in-the-ditch around each block if desired. Quilt around the leaf shapes on blocks 1, 2, 5, 6 and 7. Tie off all loose ends.

3 Stitch the binding strips with diagonal seams to make a continuous length to fit all around the quilt and use to bind the edges with a double-fold binding, mitred at the corners.

4 Add a hanging sleeve at this stage.

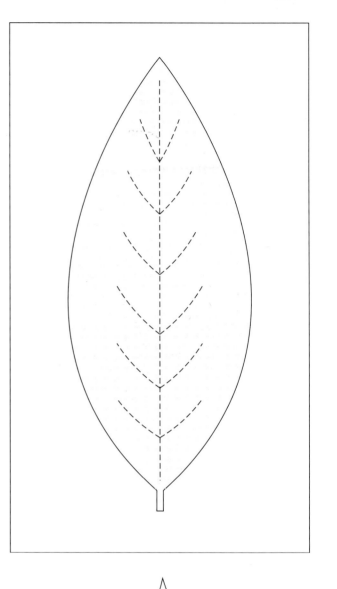

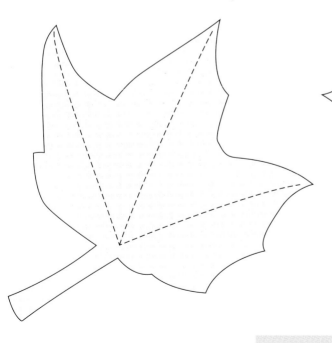

34

TEMPLATES

all 75% actual size - enlarge on
a photocopier by 133%

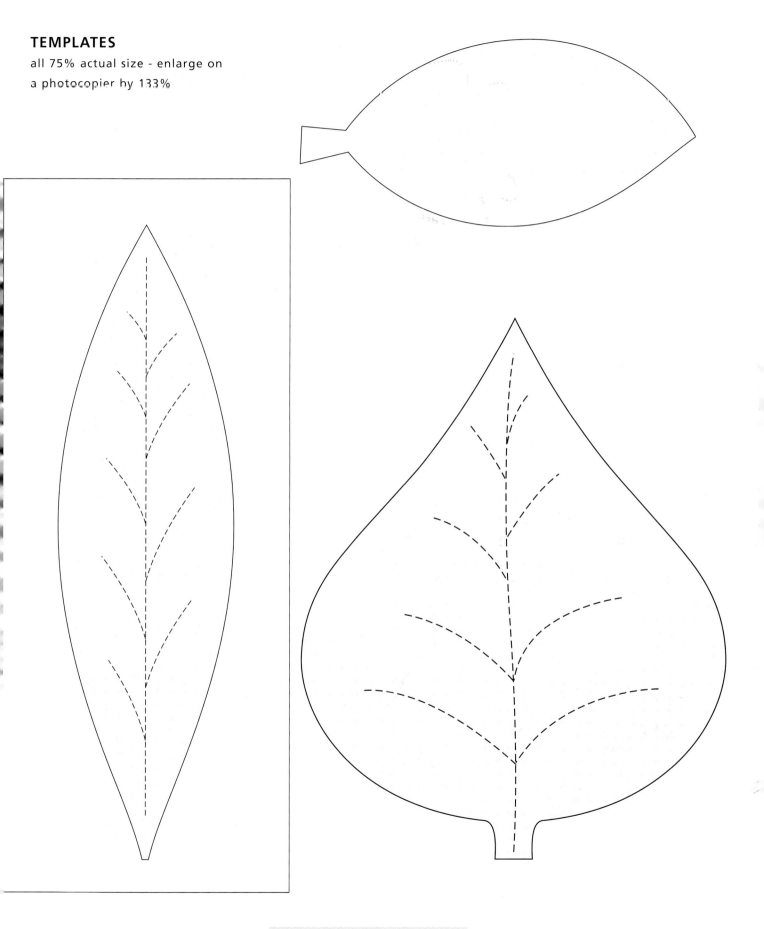

TEMPLATES

all 75% actual size -
enlarge on a photocopier
by 133%

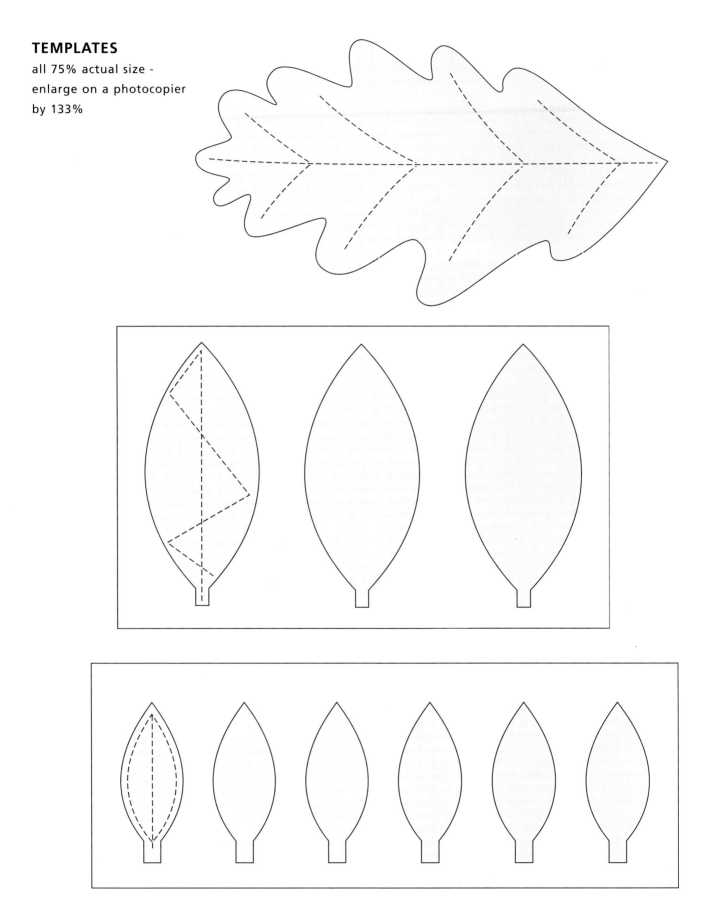

Alternative colour schemes

1 Soft flannels in warm colours to give a soft, cosy feel to the quilt; perfect for winter.
2 A warm colour scheme but with a lively green to add a bit of zing. 3 Choose fabrics
printed with a hint of metallic gold to give a rich, regal feel to the quilt. 4 This has a
more feminine feel and hints at heather in the countryside.

A Touch of Spice

DESIGNED BY

Nikki Foley

The design for this quilt was inspired by 19th-century artwork in an Indian palace. The white background with bold appliquéd shapes is complimented by gold machine-quilting, and the hand-quilted spirals capture the very essence of Indian style.

MATERIALS

All fabrics used in the quilt top are 45 in/115 cm wide, 100% cotton

Blocks and outer border: white tone on tone, 2 yds/1.75 m

Appliqué: bright pink, 10 in/25 cm; royal blue, 10 in/25 cm

Sashing and binding: turquoise, 1⅓ yds/ 1.3 m

Fusible webbing: ½ yd /0.5 m

Backing: 53 x 66 in/135 x 170 cm

Wadding: 53 x 66 in/135 x 170 cm

Quilter's pencil

Gold and turquoise threads: for machine quilting

Gold pearl cotton: for hand quilting

CUTTING

1 For the appliqué shapes, use template A on page 41 to trace 24 shapes onto the smooth side of the fusible web. Likewise, trace 12 shapes from template B, and 24 shapes from template C. Carefully cut out each shape just outside the marked lines, and place them as follows onto the wrong side of the fabrics: Template A shapes onto the pink fabric; template B and C shapes onto the royal blue fabric. Press the shapes into place. Cut out the shapes accurately along the marked lines.

2 From the white fabric, cut four strips, 12 in/31 cm deep, across the width, then cross-cut into 12 in/31 cm squares, making 12 white squares. Cut five strips 3 in/7.5 cm deep, across the width, from the remaining white fabric for the outer borders.

3 From the turquoise fabric, cut 11 strips, 2½ in/7 cm deep, across the width, for the sashing. Cross-cut six of the strips into 12 in/ 31 cm lengths to make 16 short sashing strips. Cut six strips, 2 in/5 cm wide, across the width, for the binding.

Quilt plan

Finished size: 48¹⁄₂ x 62in/125.5 x 160.5cm

STITCHING

1 Position the appliqué shapes onto the white
12 in/31 cm squares. You will need six of each
design. Align the straight edges of the royal
blue semi-circles exactly to the edges of the
white squares for incorporation into the seam
allowances (diagram 1). Peel off the paper
backing from the prepared shapes and press
in place. Stitch a decorative zig-zag, using
matching thread, around the edges of the
appliqué shapes.

diagram 1

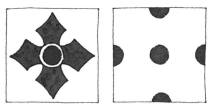

NOTE

To find the centre of each square for positioning the
appliqué shapes accurately, fold the square in half
downwards and finger press, then open and fold in half
across and again finger press. The centre will be where
the two creases meet.

2 Pin and stitch the shorter turquoise sashing
strips to each side of the white appliquéd
squares (diagram 2), right sides together, and
taking ¹⁄₄ in/0.75 cm seam allowances.
Following the quilt plan on page 40, make four
rows, alternating the pink appliqué with the
royal blue. Press all seams towards the sashing.

diagram 2

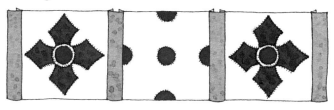

**TEMPLATES
full size**

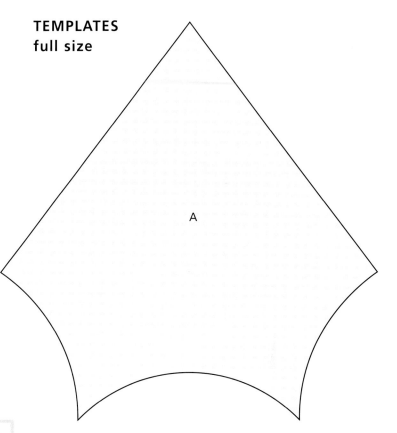

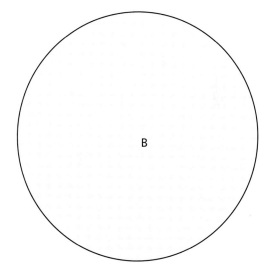

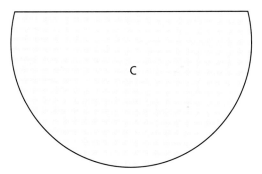

3 Pin and stitch one of the long turquoise sashing strips to the top and bottom of the first row, taking the usual seam allowances. Trim and press towards the turquoise. Pin and stitch the next row to the bottom edge of the turquoise strip. Pin and stitch another long sashing strip to the bottom of this row. Repeat to join the remaining rows with sashing strips, ending with a sashing strip. Trim and press as you go.

ADDING THE BORDERS

1 Measure the pieced top through the centre from side to side, then trim two of the white 3 in/7.5 cm border strips to this measurement. Pin and stitch to the top and bottom of the quilt.

2 Stitch the remaining white 3 in/7.5 cm border strips together. Measure the pieced top through the centre from top to bottom, then cut two strips to this measurement. Pin and stitch to the sides.

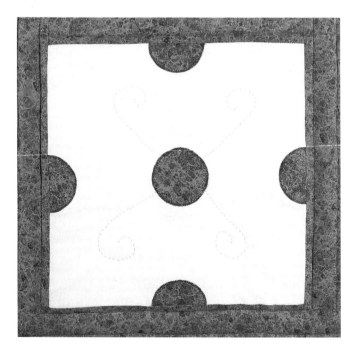

FINISHING

1 Lay the quilt top on a flat surface right side up, then, using the quilter's pencil, mark the spiral quilting design freehand on the squares appliquéd with the blue circles.

2 Spread the backing right side down on a flat surface, then smooth the wadding and place the quilt top, right side up, on the top. Fasten together with safety pins or baste in a grid.

3 Use a walking foot and gold thread to machine quilt the inside edge of each pink appliquéd square and stitch two lines of decorative stitches on either side of the border. Using a matching thread, straight stitch along the turquoise sashing. Hand quilt the spirals on each blue appliquéd square using gold pearl cotton (diagram 3).

diagram 3

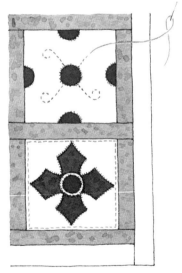

4 Trim any excess wadding and backing so they are even with the pieced top. Join the binding strips with diagonal seams to make a continuous length to fit all round the quilt and use to bind the edges with a double-fold binding, mitred at the corners.

Alternative colour schemes

1 Red, yellow and green on white background. 2 Black and white is an ideal design for a boy's room. 3 Pink and purple on a dark background create a dramatic atmosphere. 4 Pastel colours will guarantee a soft impression.

Noshi Wallhanging

DESIGNED BY

Dorothy Wood

This appliqué design is named Noshi, after the Japanese talisman that is traditionally made from strips of abalone, a seafood mollusc. The strips are tied together with pretty strips of paper and attached to gifts at New Year as an emblem of good fortune. The quilt pattern was inspired by square-panelled screens that are known in Japan as shoji, and has been designed as a picture-sized wallhanging.

MATERIALS

All fabrics used in the quilt top are 45 in/115 cm wide, 100% cotton

Appliqué: Japanese prints: four in dark-blue pattern, three in cream pattern and one in plain red, 9 x 22 in/23 x 56 cm of each

Background, sashing and binding: cream, $1\frac{1}{4}$ yds/1.1 m

Backing: 24 x 24 in/60 x 60 cm

Wadding: lightweight, 27 x 27 in/ 66.5 x 66.5 cm

Fusible webbing: 1 yd/1 m, 18 in/46 cm wide

CUTTING

1 From the cream fabric, cut nine squares, $7\frac{1}{4}$ in/18.5 cm. Cut six rectangles, 2 x $7\frac{1}{4}$ in/ 5 x 18.5 cm, and two, 2 x $23\frac{3}{4}$ in/5 x 59.5 cm, for the sashing. Cut one strip, $3\frac{1}{2}$ x 40 in/ 8.5 x 102 cm deep, across the width for the hanging tabs.

2 Enlarge the quilt templates on page 48, so that each square is $7\frac{1}{4}$ in/18.5 cm. Use the template to trace all the appliqué elements onto the smooth side of fusible web. Mark the square numbers and Japanese fabric styles on to each shape (diagram 1). Cut out the shapes just outside the marked lines.

diagram 1

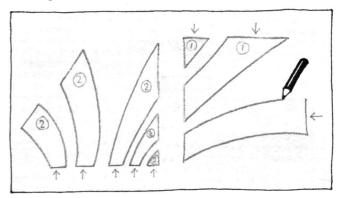

Quilt plan

Finished size: 27 x 27 in/65 x 65 cm

3 Press each fusible web shape to the wrong side of the appropriate Japanese fabric. Cut out the appliqué shapes from the fabric along the marked lines. Following the quilt plan opposite, arrange them so that the designs will flow from one square to another on the finished quilt.

STITCHING

1 Lay a square of cream fabric over each square on the template. Remove the papers from the back of the appliqué shapes and position them on the cream squares (see quilt plan). Press to secure.

2 Beginning at the edge of the pieced block, quilt in-the-ditch around each square.

3 Fold the tab strip in half along the length, right sides together. Stitch down the long side taking the usual seam allowance, then turn right side out and press with the seam in the middle. Cross-cut into four 10-in/25-cm pieces.

4 Fold over the side bindings to the reverse side and slip stitch. Lay the folded tabs with the loop facing down evenly across the top, matching the quilting lines and side borders. Pin, so that the top of the tab is level with the raw edges of the binding turning. Handstitch across the end of the tabs to secure (diagram 5).

diagram 5

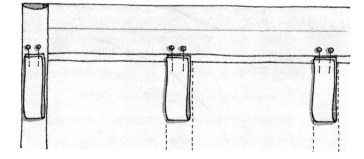

5 Fold over the top and bottom bindings to the reverse side and slip stitch. Fold the tabs up and slip stitch securely along the top edge of the quilt.

Alternative colour schemes

1 Use bold primary and secondary colours to create a bright, contemporary design. 2 Coordinating spot fabrics and toning plain fabrics would make a fun quilt. 3 Select one or two really busy prints and pick out colours from it to complete the design. 4 Choose a range of different-patterned fabrics in the same colourway.

Alternative colour schemes

1 Blue and white with a touch of silver is a fresh and cool combination. 2 Hand-dyed fabrics in hot colours make a vibrant quilt. 3 The bright green background gives a summery feel to this colourway. 4 Plain fabrics on a paint-effect background are restful.

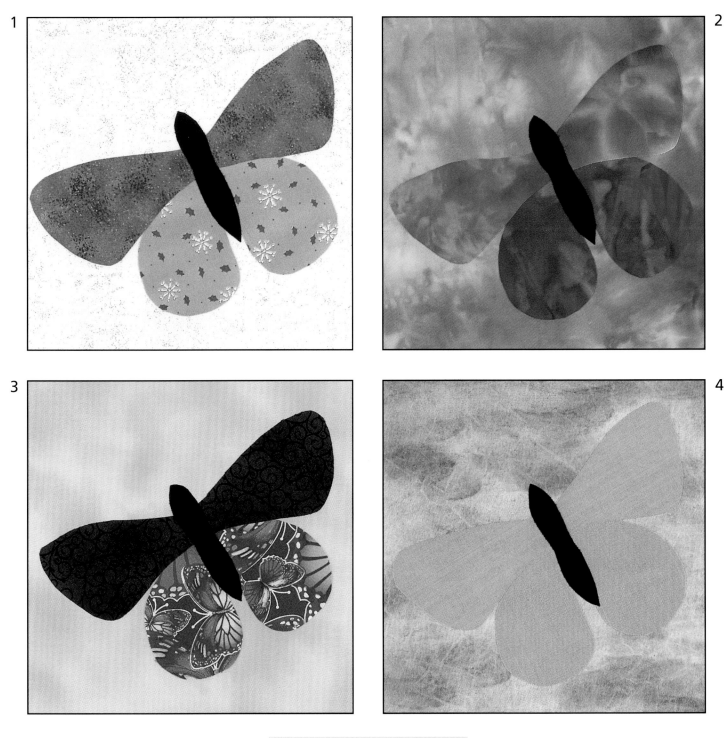

Starflower

DESIGNED BY

Mary O'Riordan

This quilt was inspired by a fabric collection containing an unusual mix of favourite colours. New and recycled fabrics have been combined to give an old-fashioned, yet exotic feel. The appliqué flowers appear to float on the surface of the quilt and are constructed from a single, simple petal shape.

MATERIALS

All fabrics used in the quilt top are 45 in/115 cm, 100% cotton

Appliqué: mauve and violet, ¼ yd/0.25 m of each

Background fabric and nine-patch blocks: pinks, mauves, pale blues and lime greens, 12 in/30 cm each of four fabrics; or scraps to total 1⅓ yds/1.25 m. I used 15 different fabrics in this quilt.

Borders and binding: cornflower blue print, 2 yds/1.75 m

Template plastic

Fusible webbing: 1 yd/1 m, 15 in/38 cm wide

Backing: 3 yds/2.75 m

Wadding: lightweight, 52 x 62 in/ 130 x 160 cm

CUTTING

1 Trace the petal template on page 62 onto template plastic and cut out accurately. Use the template to trace 30 petal shapes onto the smooth side of the fusible web and cut out allowing ¼ in/0.75 cm around the petal edges (diagram 1). Press 15 of the fusible web pieces to the wrong side of one of the appliqué fabrics and 15 to the other. Cut out the petals accurately along the marked lines to achieve six flowers, each with five petals.

diagram 1

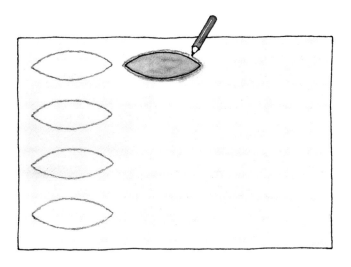

Quilt plan

Finished size: 46 x 57 in/112 x 138 cm

2 From the pinks, mauves, pale blues and lime greens, cut a total of 106 x 4 in/10 cm squares for the pieced background and nine-patch squares.

3 From the cornflower blue print, cut four strips, 11 in/27 cm deep, across the width, for the borders; cut six strips, 2 in/5 cm deep, for the binding.

STITCHING

1 Stitch four nine-patch blocks from 36 of the 4 in/10 cm squares, combining the fabrics randomly and taking $\frac{1}{4}$ in/0.75 cm seam allowances (diagram 2).

diagram 2

2 Pin and stitch the remaining 70 squares into ten rows of seven squares, taking the usual seam allowance. Then stitch the rows together, taking the usual seam allowances, to form the central background for the appliqué flowers (see quilt plan on page 60).

ADDING THE BORDERS

1 Measure the long sides of the pieced background and trim two border strips to this measurement. Pin and stitch these to the long sides, taking the usual seam allowance.

2 Trim the remaining two border strips to measure 25 in/61 cm and stitch a nine-patch block to each end. Then pin and stitch these rows to the top and bottom, taking the usual seam allowance and matching seams carefully (diagram 3).

diagram 3

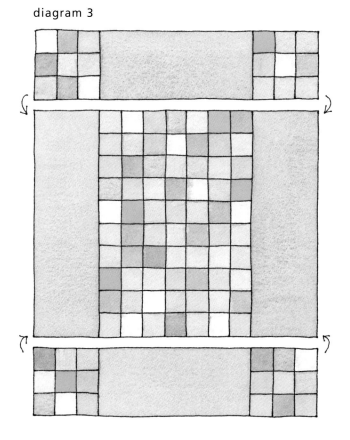

TEMPLATE full size

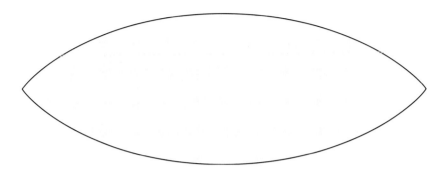

FINISHING

1 Peel off the paper backing from the prepared petals and position as desired on the quilt top. Press in place. Stitch a small decorative zig-zag, using matching thread, around the petal shapes as close as possible to the edge.

2 Spread the backing right side down on a flat surface, then smooth out the wadding and the pieced top, right side up, on top. Fasten together with safety pins or baste in a grid.

3 Beginning at the edge of the pieced block, machine or hand quilt in a grid on the background squares and outline the star flowers. Quilt the border in a continuous vine pattern.

4 Stitch the binding strips with diagonal seams to make a continuous length to fit all around the quilt and use to bind the edges with a double-fold binding, mitred at the corners.

Alternative colour schemes

1 Rich autumnal red- and rust-coloured fabric with leaves in golds and browns would make this quilt perfect for hibernation! **2** Use scraps of black and white and a different fabric for each petal, for a happy, scrappy quilt. **3** A neutral background will work with almost any favourite fabric for this buttercup and blue scheme. **4** Recycled checks and the latest batiks are combined in a low-contrast colour scheme.

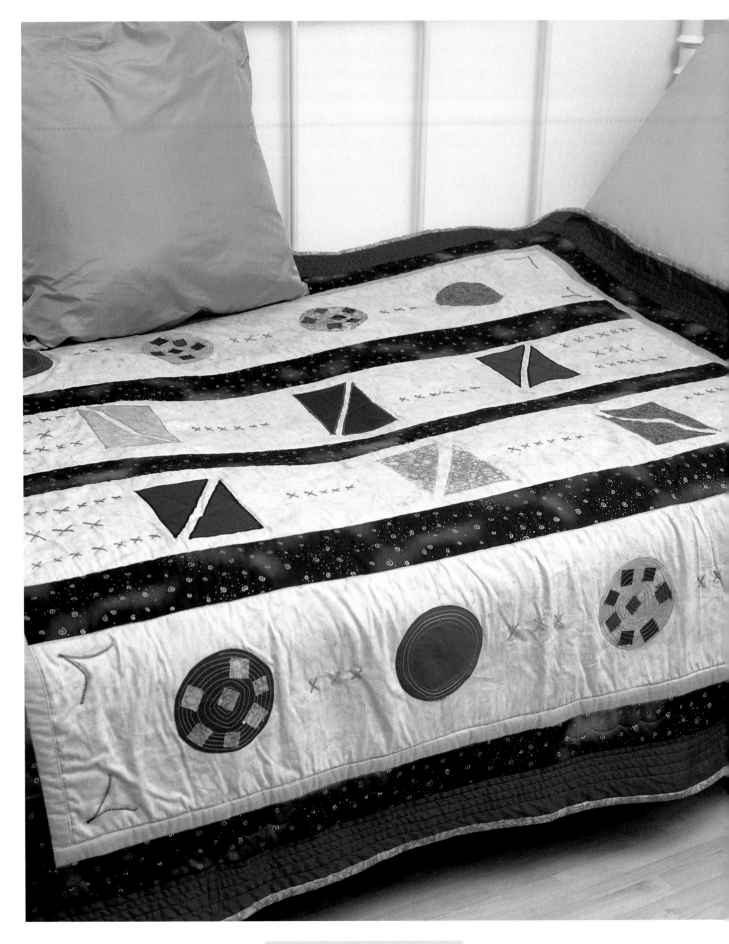

Promenade Throw

DESIGNED BY

Gail Smith

This throw features silk, velvet and fleece, those luxurious fabrics that are not normally used in patchwork. The design comes from a waistcoat I originally created for my daughter as part of an embroidery project, and is inspired by the parasols, beach huts and the seashells that are found at the seaside. The raw-edge appliqué adds additional luxury, while the hand and machine embroidery give further interest. The shape of the throw is perfect for a sofa or futon.

MATERIALS

The cotton, silk and velvet used in the quilt top are 45 in/115 cm wide. The fleece fabric is 60 in/153 cm wide

Background panels: pink batik, 1 yd/1 m

Sashing and second border: royal blue, 24 in/60 cm

First and outer borders: turquoise cotton lamé, 6 in/15 cm; cerise silk, 20 in/50 cm

Appliqué: 6 different fabrics in cerise, blue, turquoise and pink in assorted materials, such as silk, velvet and cotton, 9 x 22 in/25 x 56 cm of each

Fusible webbing: 1 yd/1 m, 15 in/38 cm wide

Backing: pink fleece, 1½ yds/1.5 m

Binding: dark pink floral batik, 8 in/20 cm

Pearl cotton thread: pink/blue variegated for embroidery

CUTTING

1 From the pink batik fabric, cut four strips, 8½ in/21.5 cm deep, across the width, for the main panels.

2 From the royal blue fabric, cut three strips, 3½ in/9 cm deep, across the width, for the sashing. Cut four strips, 2½ in/6.5 cm deep, across the width, for the second border.

3 From the turquoise cotton lamé, cut four strips, 1¼ in/3.5 cm deep, across the width for the inner border.

4 From the cerise silk, cut four strips, 3½ in/9 cm deep, across the width, for the outer border.

5 From the dark pink floral batik, cut five strips, 1½ in/4 cm deep, across the width, for the binding.

Quilt plan

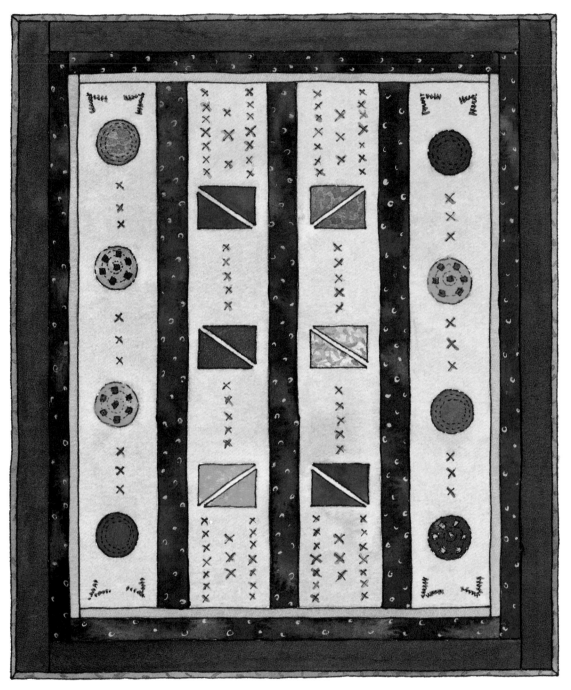

Finished size: 47 x 55 in/116 x 140 cm

STITCHING

1 Remove the papers from the back of the appliqué circles and triangles and position them, right side up, on the pink panels following the quilt plan on page 66. Press in place. Remove the papers from the backs of the small squares of velvet and silk and press onto the circles in a random pattern (add more small squares if you wish).

2 With matching thread, stitch a spiral pattern onto each circle. Use the markings on the presser foot as a guide, and starting at the outer edge, stitch until you reach the centre point. On the circles with velvet and silk decorative squares, catch these down as you stitch the spirals (diagram 2). You may wish to practise on a sample first.

diagram 2

> **NOTE**
>
> If the silk fabric for the borders starts to fray, you may wish to prevent this by neatening the edges with an overlock stitch. Any other silk fabric shapes will not fray once the fusible webbing has been applied to them.

6 Use the template patterns on page 69 to trace eight circles and six rectangles onto the smooth side of the fusible web. Cut out the shapes just outside the marked lines (diagram 1).

diagram 1

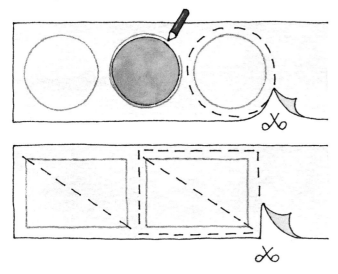

7 Press the fusible web shapes onto the wrong side of the assorted appliqué fabrics. Cut out the shapes following accurately the marked lines on the fusible web. Cut the rectangles in half diagonally to make 12 triangles.

8 Apply fusible web to the wrong side of the silk and velvet to be used to decorate the appliqué circles in order to prevent fraying. Roughly cut 32 x ³/₄ in/2 cm squares to decorate four of the appliqué circles.

3 Stitch zig-zag around the edges of the triangles, using matching thread. Neaten the back of the panels by taking threads to the back and stitching in as necessary.

4 Trim the four panels to 42½ in/107 cm, and position the panels to align the appliqué patterns.

5 Pin and stitch the three royal-blue sashing strips between the four pink panels, right sides together, and taking a ¼ in/0.75 cm seam allowance. Press the seams towards the darker fabric. Trim level with the panels.

TEMPLATES
full size

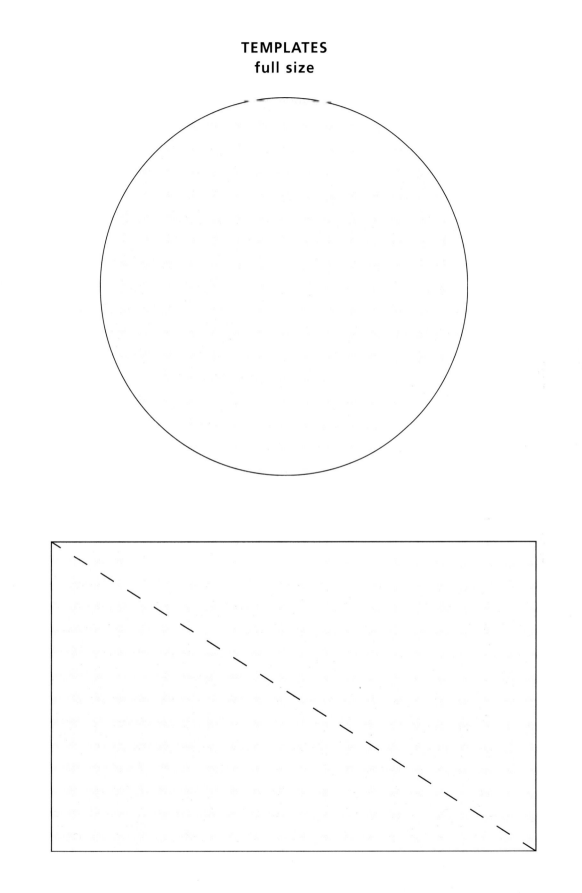

ADDING THE BORDERS

1 Measure the pieced top through the centre from side to side, then cut two of the turquoise border strips to this measurement. Pin and stitch to the top and bottom of the quilt.

2 Measure the pieced top through the centre from top to bottom, then cut two turquoise border strips to this measurement. Pin and stitch to the sides.

3 Add the second border in the same way. Measure the pieced top through the centre from side to side, then cut two strips to this measurement. Pin and stitch to the top and bottom of the quilt. Measure the top through the centre from top to bottom, then cut two strips to this measurement. Pin and stitch to the sides.

4 Next, attach the outer border: pin and stitch two of the cerise strips together. Measure the pieced top through the centre from side to side, then cut two strips to this measurement. Pin and stitch to the top and bottom of the quilt. Stitch the remaining cerise strips together. Measure the top through the centre from top to bottom, then cut two strips to this measurement. Pin and stitch to the sides.

5 Press all the seams towards the darker fabrics. Note that silk and cotton lamé need to be pressed at a lower temperature than cotton.

FINISHING

1 Using pearl cotton thread and a crewel needle (sharp point, large eye – I used variegated No. 5), stitch large decorative cross-stitches on the panels (see quilt plan). Secure with small back stitches on the rear of the panels. Machine embroider at the ends of the two outer pink panels as desired (see quilt plan).

2 Measure the pieced top and trim the backing fleece to ½ in/1.5 cm larger all around. Spread the fleece backing right side down on a flat surface, then smooth out the pieced top, right side up, on top. Fasten together with safety pins or baste in a grid.

3 Use a walking foot and a straight stitch, quilt in-the-ditch around the main panels.

4 Quilt a decorative wave stitch along the royal-blue sashing strips and in the royal-blue border.

5 Add decorative stitches to the appliqué triangles as shown on the quilt plan.

6 On the outer cerise border, straight stitch four parallel rows at slightly wider measure apart each time.

7 Stitch the binding strips with diagonal seams to make a continuous length to fit all around the quilt and use to bind the edges with a double-fold binding, mitred at the corners.

Alternative colour schemes

1 Hot colours suitable for a neutral colour scheme. 2 Blue-green and yellow produce a more masculine look. Batik fabrics have been used for the appliqué. 3 A sophisticated scheme, reminiscent of a winter's day with ice and snow. 4 Lime green and pink are perfect colours for a young girl, a modern colour scheme or if you just like pink!

Tumbling Bows

DESIGNED BY

Dorothy Wood

Shadow appliqué is one of the quickest methods of appliqué. The pieces are simply sandwiched between a sheer fabric and the quilt top, then machined with straight stitch. The fabrics appear paler underneath the sheer fabric and so bold colours are best used for the appliqué pieces.

MATERIALS

All the white fabrics in this quilt are 59 in/150 cm wide. Coloured fabrics are 45 in/115 cm wide

Background and backing: white cotton, 2¾ yds/2.4 m

Binding, border squares, triangles: striped fabric, 1½ yds/1.4 m; lilac, blue, green pastel fabrics, fat quarter (18 x 22 in/50 x 55 cm) of each; lilac, blue, green bold fabrics, 6 x 12 in/15 x 30 cm of each

Quilt top: white sheer fabric, 37 x 45 in/94 x 114 cm

Wadding: lightweight, 45 x 54 in/114 x 137 cm

Fusible webbing: 18 x 24 in/46 x 61 cm

Template card

Large piece of paper, at least 36 x 44 in/90 x 110 cm

Fine black indelible pen

Quilt marking pen

Pale green stranded embroidery cotton

CUTTING

1 From the white background fabric, cut out a rectangle, 36½ x 44½ in/91.5 x 111.5 cm, for the quilt top and another rectangle, 45 x 53 in/114 x 134 cm, for the backing.

2 From the striped fabric, cut two strips, 1¼ x 52 in/3 x 132 cm, down the length, and two strips, 1¼ x 43 in/3 x 109 cm, for the binding. Cut 22 x 4½ in/11.5 cm squares.

3 From the pastel fabrics, cut eight lilac, seven blue and seven green 4½ in/11.5 cm squares.

4 Trace the triangle template on page 75 on to stiff card and cut out. Draw 32 triangles on to the smooth side of the fusible web in rows of four, allowing at least ¼ in/0.75 cm between the shapes. Cut around the shapes just outside the pencil lines.

Quilt plan

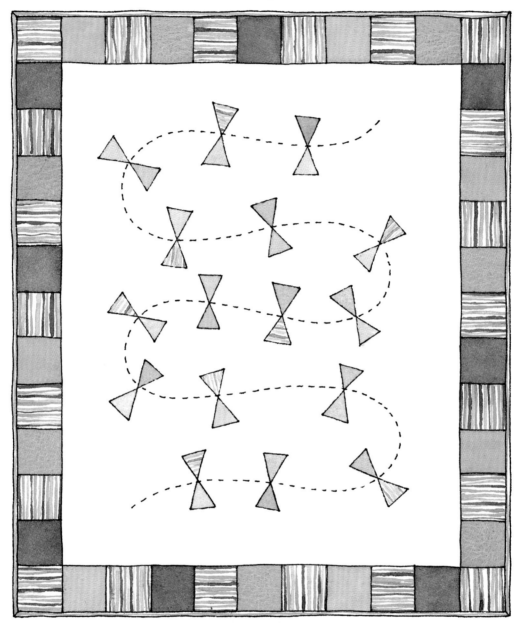

Finished size: 45 x 53 in/114 x 134 cm

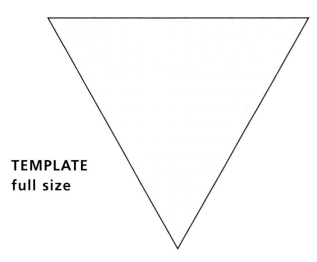

**TEMPLATE
full size**

5 To make 32 triangles, press one set of four
triangles on to each of the pastel fabrics, one
set of four onto each of the bold fabrics and
two sets of four triangles on to the striped
fabric, arranging the first so that the stripes
are horizontal and the second so that the
lines are vertical (diagram 1). Cut out all
triangles following the marked lines.

diagram 1

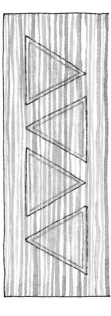

STITCHING

1 Enlarge the quilt pattern shown in diagram
2). To do this, draw a 36 x 44 in/90 x 110 cm
rectangle on a large piece of paper. Mark the
rectangle into a grid of 4 in/10 cm squares.
Transfer the pattern on to the paper one
square at a time, using the fine black indelible pen. Use the triangle card template to
mark the bows.

diagram 2

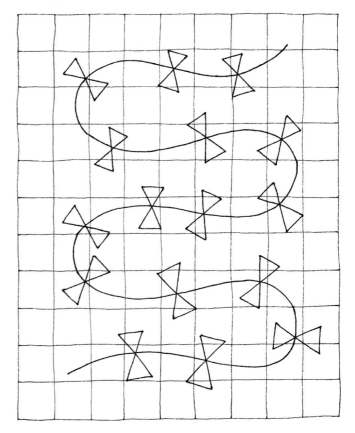

2 Pin the background fabric over the pattern
and, using the quilt marking pen, trace the
design onto the fabric. You need only mark a
cross to show the position and direction of
each bow.

3 Remove the papers from the fabric triangles
and position them, right side up, on the background fabric following the pattern. Press on
the right side and on the reverse to secure.

4 Lay the sheer fabric over the top on the right side and baste across the middle in both directions and around the outside edge.

ADDING THE BORDERS

1 Following the quilt plan on page 74, stitch the 22 x 4½ in/11.5 cm striped squares, and the 22 x 4½ in/11.5 cm pastel squares together to make the borders (diagram 3). The top and bottom of the quilt will require nine squares, and each side border will require 13 squares. Take ¼ in/0.75 cm seam allowances and press the seams towards the darker colours.

diagram 3

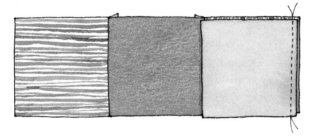

2 Pin the shorter strips to the top and bottom edges of the centre panel. Measure to check that the side border strips will fit exactly. If necessary, trim the centre panel to fit, then stitch the top and bottom borders in place, taking a 1¼ in/ 0.75cm seam allowance. Press the seams towards the borders.

3 Pin the side borders in place being careful to match seams. Stitch and press as above.

FINISHING

1 Spread the backing right side down on a flat surface, then smooth out the wadding and the quilt top, right side up, on top. Insert pins about ½ in/1 cm from the ends of each bow (diagram 4). Baste along the marked curved line. This holds the fabric in exactly the right place for the hand quilting.

diagram 4

2 Machine stitch around each bow, overlapping the stitching slightly where the ends meet (diagram 4).

3 Quilt in-the-ditch around the inner edge of the border. Machine stitch between each of the squares, reverse stitching at the inner edge to secure the threads. Trim all thread ends.

4 Using three strands of embroidery cotton, work running stitch through all three layers along the marked curved line. Begin and finish each length with small back stitches on the reverse side.

5 Join the binding strips with diagonal seams to make a continuous length to fit all round the quilt and use to bind the edges with a double-fold binding, mitred at the corners.

Alternative colour schemes

1 Use pastel gingham fabrics and a baby print to make a cot quilt. **2** Choose a pretty print and pick out pale shades for the border and bold colours for the bows. **3** Make an even bolder quilt by using strong colours for both the border and the appliqué. **4** Contemporary print fabrics can suggest an unusual and vibrant colour scheme.

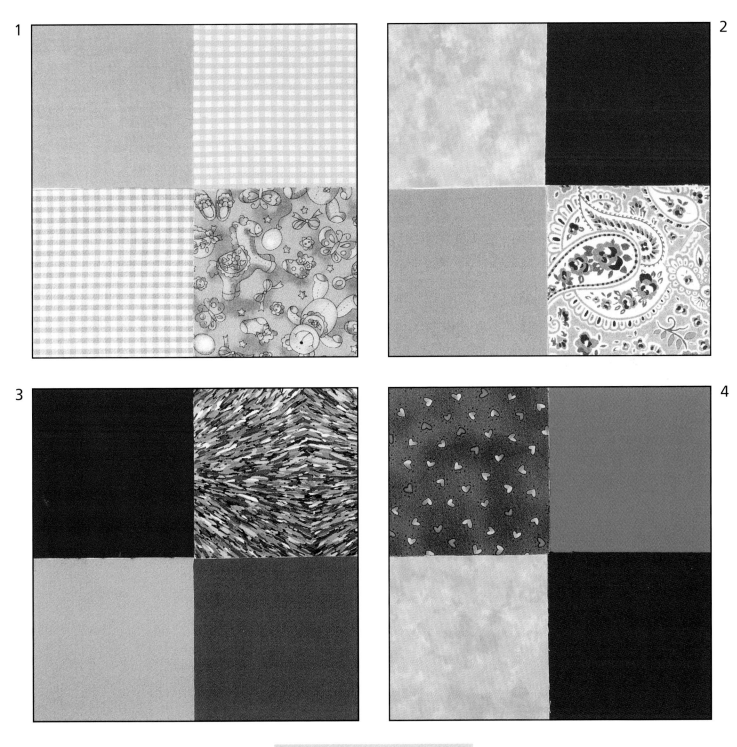

Hawaiian Snowflakes

DESIGNED BY

Sarah Wellfair

This quilt uses the Hawaiian appliqué technique for which both the piece cut out and the background from which it was cut are used in the design. A clever, quick way of producing the nine snowflakes that make up this festive throw.

MATERIALS

All fabrics used in the quilt top are 45 in/115 cm wide, 100% cotton

Snowflakes, outer borders and binding: purple, $1\frac{1}{2}$ yds/1.4 m

Blocks and inner borders: cream, $1\frac{1}{2}$ yds/1.4 m

Binding: purple, 12 in/30 cm

Fusible webbing: 55 in/135 cm, 15 in/38 cm wide

Backing: cream, 50 in/125 cm

Wadding: lightweight, a piece 50 in/125 cm square

CUTTING

1 From the purple fabric, cut two strips, $10\frac{1}{2}$ in/26.5 cm deep, across the width, then cross-cut into five $10\frac{1}{2}$ in/26.5 cm squares, for the blocks; cut four strips, $2\frac{1}{2}$ in/6 cm deep, across the width, for the inner borders; cut strips, 3 in/7.5 cm deep, across the width, for the binding.

2 From the cream fabric, cut three strips, $10\frac{1}{2}$ in/26.5 cm deep, across the width, then cross-cut into ten $10\frac{1}{2}$ in/26.5 cm squares, for the blocks; cut four strips, $4\frac{1}{2}$ in/11.5 cm deep, across the width, for the outer borders.

3 From the fusible web, cut out five $10\frac{1}{2}$ in/26.5 cm squares. Use the snowflake template on page 82 to trace the pattern onto the centre of the smooth side of these squares. Position the fusible web squares wrong side down on the reverse of the purple fabric squares and press to bond.

4 Using small sharp-pointed scissors, start cutting out the snowflake shape at one of the points of the snowflake (see note on page 81). Cut all round the shape to produce a background snowflake shape and a snowflake shape: both will be used for the appliqué (see diagram 1). Make five of each.

diagram 1

Quilt plan

Finished size: 42½ x 42½ in/105.5 x 105.5 cm

NOTE

To make it easier to start cutting out the snowflake shapes, use pointed-end scissors and fold the shape in half, then make a small snip at one flake tip and insert the scissor points (diagram 2). Open out and continue cutting round the shape.

diagram 2

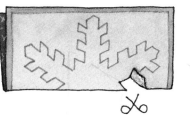

STITCHING

1 Take one cream square and place a purple snowflake shape right side up on top, ensuring that it is positioned centrally. Remove the paper from the back of the snowflake and press in place, right side up.

2 Take the corresponding purple background shape and position right side up on top of another cream background square, aligning all raw edges. Remove the paper from the back and press into position. Repeat with the remaining snowflakes and background snowflake shapes to make nine squares in total (the extra square can be set aside for machine appliquéing practice).

3 Stitch a small zig-zag around the edges of the snowflakes: on the cream squares, appliqué the outer edges of the snowflake outline; on the purple squares, appliqué the inner edges of the snowflake outline.

4 Following the quilt plan on page 80, position the snowflake blocks, alternating cream and purple, and stitch them in rows of three, right

sides together and taking a $\frac{1}{4}$ in/0.75 cm seam allowance. Join the rows together, again right sides together and taking the usual seam allowance. Press the seams towards the darker fabrics.

ADDING THE BORDERS

1 Measure the pieced top through the centre from side to side, then trim two of the $2\frac{1}{2}$ in/6 cm purple border strips to this measurement. Pin and stitch to the top and bottom of the quilt.

2 Measure the pieced top through the centre from top to bottom, then cut the two remaining purple border strips to this measurement. Pin and stitch to the sides.

3 Repeat steps 1 and 2 using the $4\frac{1}{2}$ in/11.5 cm cream border strips to add the outer borders.

FINISHING

1 Trim the backing and wadding 2 in/5 cm larger than the pieced top. Spread the backing right side down on a flat surface, then smooth out the wadding and the pieced top, right side up, on top. Fasten together with safety pins or baste in a grid.

2 Free-motion quilt with gold metallic thread and an 80/12 metallic needle around the snowflakes on the cream backgrounds and quilt in your own chosen pattern in the cream borders. Trim the excess wadding and backing to the edge of the borders.

3 Stitch the binding strips with diagonal seams to make a continuous length to fit all around the quilt, and use to bind the edges with a double-fold binding, mitred at the corners.

TEMPLATE
full size

Alternative colour schemes

1 Red and white make a striking combination. 2 Frosty blue and buttery yellow give a softer colour scheme. 3 Dark blue with light blue and silver are dramatic and sparkling. 4 Christmas holly and red make a really festive quilt.

Flowering Chains

DESIGNED BY

Janet Goddard

A cheery quilt is made from fabric scraps of many colours and patterns. It is constructed from two repeating blocks — a chain block and a simple appliquéd flower block. The layout of the quilt produces a secondary pattern of crossing lines.

MATERIALS

All fabrics used in the quilt are
45 in/115 cm wide, 100% cotton

Background squares: cream, 2 yds/1.75 m

Chain blocks, appliqué blocks, flower heads and centres: varied fabric scraps, 2¼ yds/2 m in total. The minimum size for the squares is 20 in/52 cm and for the flower heads, 2¼ in/6 cm. At least 10 different fabrics are needed to give two variations on the chain block.

Appliqué: green for stems and leaves, 10 in/25 cm

Borders and binding: bright blue, 1¼ yds/1.1 m

Wadding: lightweight 80%/20% cotton/polyester, 60 x 80 in/152.5 x 203 cm

Backing: bright blue, 60 x 80 in/152.5 x 203 cm

Fusible webbing: 20 in/50 cm wide; 1¼ yds/1 m

CUTTING

1 For each of the 18 chain blocks you require five different patterned fabrics plus the cream background fabric.
For one chain block cut the following:
Scrap fabric 1: four 2½in/6.5 cm squares
Scrap fabric 2: eight 2½ in/6.5 cm squares
Scrap fabric 3: four 2½ in/6.5 cm squares
Scrap fabric 4: four 2½ in/6.5 cm squares
Scrap fabric 5: one 2½ in/6.5 cm square
Background fabric: four 2½ in/6.5 cm squares.

NOTE

Choose the fabrics for each block randomly rather than deliberating too carefully about whether the fabrics work together. As you can see from my quilt, the fabrics are stitched together in a riot of colour.

2 For each one of the 17 appliquéd blocks cut the following:
Background fabric: one 6½ in/16.5 cm square and four 2½ x 6½ in/6.5 x 16.5 cm rectangles
Scrap fabric: four 2½ in/6.5 cm squares

Quilt plan

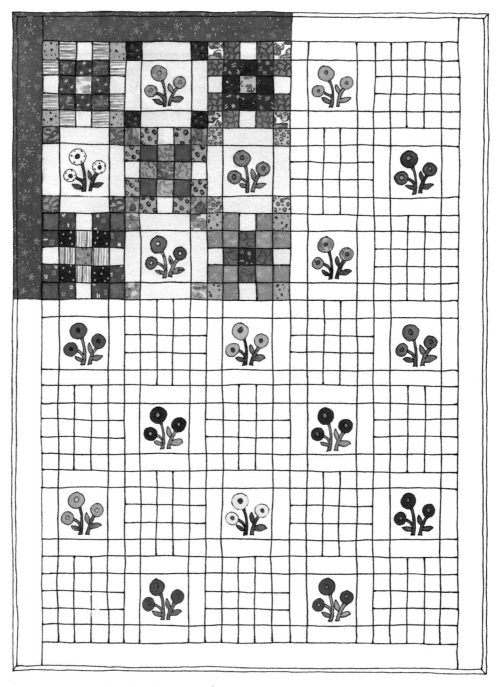

Finished size: 56$\frac{1}{2}$ x 77 in/141.5 x 193 cm

3 Use the templates on page 87 to trace 17 sets of the stems, leaves, flower heads and flower centres onto the smooth side of the fusible web. Cut out the shapes just outside the marked lines. Press the shapes for the stems and leaves to the wrong side of the green fabric, and the shapes for the flower heads and centres to the wrong side of some remaining fabric scraps.

TEMPLATES
full size

4 Cut out the sets of appliqué shapes following accurately the marked lines on the fusible web papers.

5 From the bright blue fabric, cut seven strips, 3½ in/9 cm deep, across the width, for the borders; cut seven strips, 2 in/5 cm deep, across the width, for the binding.

STITCHING

Each finished chain block measures 10½ in/26.5 cm square.

1 Lay out the fabric squares in the order shown in diagram 1.

2 Stitch the squares together first in horizontal rows, right sides together and taking a ¼ in/0.75 cm seam allowance. Press the seams in the first row to the right, then stitch the

second row and press the seams to the left. Repeat this for all rows. Stitch the rows together. Press.

3 Repeat to stitch 18 chain blocks in total.

Each finished appliqué block measures 10½ in/26.5 cm square.

fabric pieces in the order shown

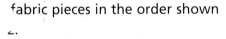

diagram 1   diagram 2

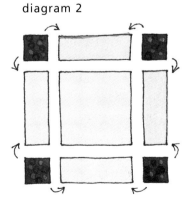

5 Stitch a fabric scrap 2½ in/6.5 cm square to each end of a background rectangle, taking the usual seam allowance. Press the seams towards the squares.

6 Stitch a background rectangle to each side of a 6½ in/16.5 cm background square, taking the usual seam allowance. Press the seams towards the centre.

7 Stitch the top and bottom rows to the centre row, taking the usual seam allowance. Press.

8 Remove the papers from the back of the stems, leaves and flower fabrics and position them in the centre of each appliqué block (diagram 3). Press to bond the fabrics and zig-zag stitch around each shape, matching threads to fabrics.

diagram 3

9 Stitch and appliqué 17 blocks in total.

10 Following the quilt plan on page 86, lay out the blocks in seven rows of five blocks, alternating chain and appliqué blocks. The first row begins with a chain block, the second row begins with an appliqué block and so on.

11 Stitch the blocks together in horizontal rows, taking the usual seam allowance. Press the seams in the first row to the right, and the seams in the second row to the left. Press the seams alternately right or left for all rows.

12 Stitch the rows together, taking the usual seam allowance. Press.

ADDING THE BORDERS

1 Stitch the seven border strips together into one long strip. Measure the pieced top through the centre from side to side, then cut two strips from the strip to this measurement. Pin and stitch to the top and bottom of the quilt.

2 Measure the pieced top through the centre from top to bottom, then cut two more strips to this measurement. Pin and stitch to the sides.

FINISHING

1 Spread the backing right side down on a flat surface, then smooth out the wadding and the pieced top, right side up, on top. Fasten together with safety pins or baste in a grid.

2 Use cream thread to quilt ½ in/1 cm from the seam line around each appliqué block, extending the quilting into the small background squares of the adjoining chain blocks (diagram 4).

diagram 4

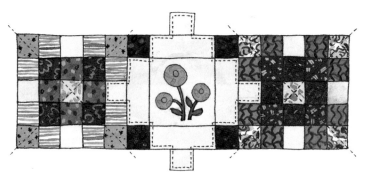

3 Use invisible thread to quilt on both diagonals through each chain block (diagram 4).

4 Stitch the binding strips with diagonal seams to make a continuous length to fit all around the quilt and use to bind the edges with a double-fold binding, mitred at the corners.

Alternative colour schemes

1 and 3 Two blocks show the quilt stitched entirely in fabrics of a single colour group, such as purples and lilacs. 2 and 4 Two blocks showing the effect achieved with a dark background fabric.

Summer Garden

DESIGNED BY

Jane Coombes

I have always been attracted to the traditional "Log Cabin" block and its variations. This quilt is based on a variation called "Courthouse Steps" for which I have used just two rounds of steps in order to create sufficient space for the appliqué. The appliqué designs are on the theme of a summer garden: cottages, trees, flowers and birds. The bright colours used also reflect summer although, if you prefer more muted tones, these could be changed to autumnal colours and the flowers made in yellow and brown to depict sunflowers and the coming of harvest time.

MATERIALS

All fabrics used in the quilt top are 45 in/115 cm wide, 100% cotton

Centre squares: pale purple, 20 in/50 cm

Strips, appliqué, borders and binding: mid-purple, 36 in/90 cm; pink, 30 in/75 cm; deep purple (main colour), 50 in/1.25 m

Backing: one piece, 44 x 60 in/ 112 x 150 cm

Wadding: lightweight, 44 x 60 in/ 112 x 150 cm

Fusible webbing: 12 x 18 in/35 x 50 cm

Stabilizer: 9 x 36 in/25 x 90 cm

Decorative machine embroidery thread

CUTTING

1 From the pale purple fabric, cut three strips, 4 in/10 cm deep, across the width, then cross-cut into 24 x 4 in/10 cm squares.

2 From the mid-purple fabric, cut 15 strips, 1½ in/4 cm deep, across the width, then cross-cut into 24 x 8 in/20 cm strips, 48 x 6 in/15 cm strips, and 24 x 4 in/10 cm strips.

3 From the pink fabric, cut 15 strips, 1½ in/4 cm deep, across the width, then cross-cut into 24 x 8 in/20 cm strips, 48 x 6 in/15 cm strips, and 24 x 4 in/10 cm strips.

NOTE

Stack each length strip of both colours into six piles on your work surface to help with methodical piecing.

Quilt plan

Finished size: 38 x 53 in/92.5 x 131 cm

4 From the deep purple fabric, cut five strips, 4 in/10 cm deep, across the width, for the borders; cut five strips, 2¼ in/6 cm deep, for the binding.

NOTE

For a professional finish, use the arrows on the templates to align the appliqué shape with the straight grain of the fabric.

---

5 For the appliqué shapes, trace the templates on pages 94 and 95 on to the smooth side of the fusible web.
For the birds, you will need two of each; cut out the fusible web shapes just outside the marked lines. Press the shapes to the wrong side of the remaining mid-purple fabric.
For the flowers, you will need eight petal and eight centre shapes. Cut out the fusible web shapes outside the marked lines, and press the petal shapes to the wrong side of the deep purple fabric, and the centre shapes to the pink fabric.
For the trees, trace eight trunks and eight foliage shapes. Cut out the fusible web shapes outside the marked lines, and press the trunk shapes on to the deep purple fabric; press the foliage shapes on to the mid-purple fabric.
For the cottages, trace four of each of the door, roof and wall shapes, and eight of the window shapes. Cut out the fusible web shapes outside the marked lines and press the wall shapes on to the mid-purple fabric; the roof and door shapes onto the deep purple and the window shapes onto the pink.

6 Cut out all the appliqué shapes accurately following the marked lines on the fusible web papers.

STITCHING

1 Stitch one 4 in/10 cm mid-purple strip to the top of one 4 in/10 cm pale purple centre square, right sides together and taking a ¼ in/0.75 cm seam allowance (diagram 1a). Then stitch one 4 in/10 cm pink strip to the bottom of the square, taking the usual seam allowance (diagram 1b). Press the seams towards the strips.

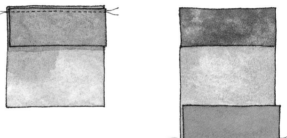

diagram 1a   diagram 1b

2 Following diagram 2, add one 6 in/15 cm mid-purple strip (3) and one 6 in/15 cm pink strip (4) to either side of the central square, taking the usual seam allowances. Press the seams towards the strips. Stitch another 6 in/15 cm mid-purple strip (5) and another 6 in/15 cm pink strip (6) to the top and bottom of this unit. Press as before.

diagram 2

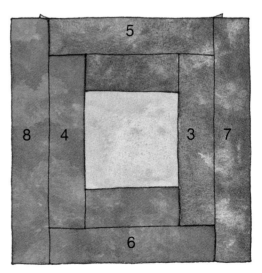

TEMPLATES
all full size

**arrows indicate direction of
straight grain of fabric**

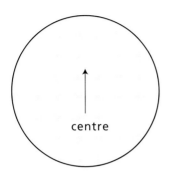

centre

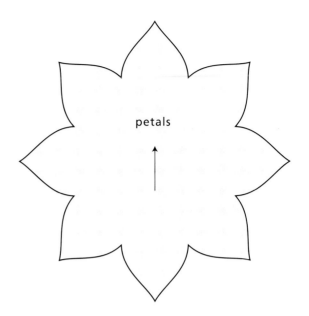

petals

3 Stitch an 8 in/10 cm mid-purple strip (7) to one side and an 8 in/10 cm pink strip (8) to the opposite side. Press as before. This completes one Courthouse Steps block. Repeat with the remaining 23 blocks.

4 To assemble the appliqué, follow the quilt plan on page 92 and lay out the blocks in six rows of four blocks, noting which way the

longer seams are laid to achieve the secondary colour sequence. Mark the top of each block with a pin to ensure the appliqué is worked the right way up.

5 Remove the backing papers from the appliqué shapes and with right sides up, position each shape in its appropriate square and press in place.

6 To stabilize the background before stitching, pin a 3 in/8 cm square of stabilizer (such as Stitch 'n Tear™) to the wrong side of the block, covering the area behind the appliqué shape. Machine stitch in place using a zig-zag, satin or decorative stitch as desired.

7 Remove the stabilizer and press on the wrong side.

8 Reassemble the blocks following the quilt plan. Stitch the blocks into six rows, taking the usual seam allowances. Press the seams alternately, i.e., press the first row to the left, the second to the right, third to the left, and so on. This will assist accurate matching of seams when the rows are joined.

9 Pin and stitch the rows together to complete the pieced top, taking the usual seam allowances and matching seams carefully. Press the seams towards the bottom of the quilt.

ADDING THE BORDERS

1 Stitch three of the five deep purple border strips together across the short ends. Measure the pieced top through the centre from top to bottom, then cut two strips to this measurement from the joined strip. Stitch to the sides of the quilt. Press the seams towards the borders.

2 Measure the pieced top through the centre from side to side, then trim the remaining two strips to this measurement. Stitch to the top and bottom of the quilt and press the seams as before.

FINISHING

1 Spread the backing right side down on a flat surface, then smooth out the wadding and the pieced top, right side up, on top. Fasten together with safety pins or baste in a grid.

2 Machine or hand quilt in-the-ditch around the blocks to emphasize the design of the patchwork. Use an invisible thread on the top and a thread to match the backing fabric in the bobbin. Embellish the blocks by machine stitching a decorative embroidery stitch in curved lines first around the central pink cross shape, then around both the purple and pink diamond shapes. A curved border design can be machine stitched on the border.

3 Join the binding strips with diagonal seams to make a continuous length to fit all round the quilt and use to bind the edges with a double-fold binding, mitred at the corners.

NOTE

Use a walking/even-feed foot on your sewing machine when stitching through three or more layers to prevent tucks on the underneath fabrics.

Alternative colour schemes

1, 2 and 3 The design is based on the use of a light, medium and dark shade of one colour with a medium shade of a strong contrasting colour. Here are 3 further examples of the use of differing shades. **4** Try using three primary colours plus green for a bright nursery quilt. *Note*: If time is short or you do not want to work the appliqué, simply use a novelty fabric for the block centres and select colours that complement this for the surrounding fabrics.

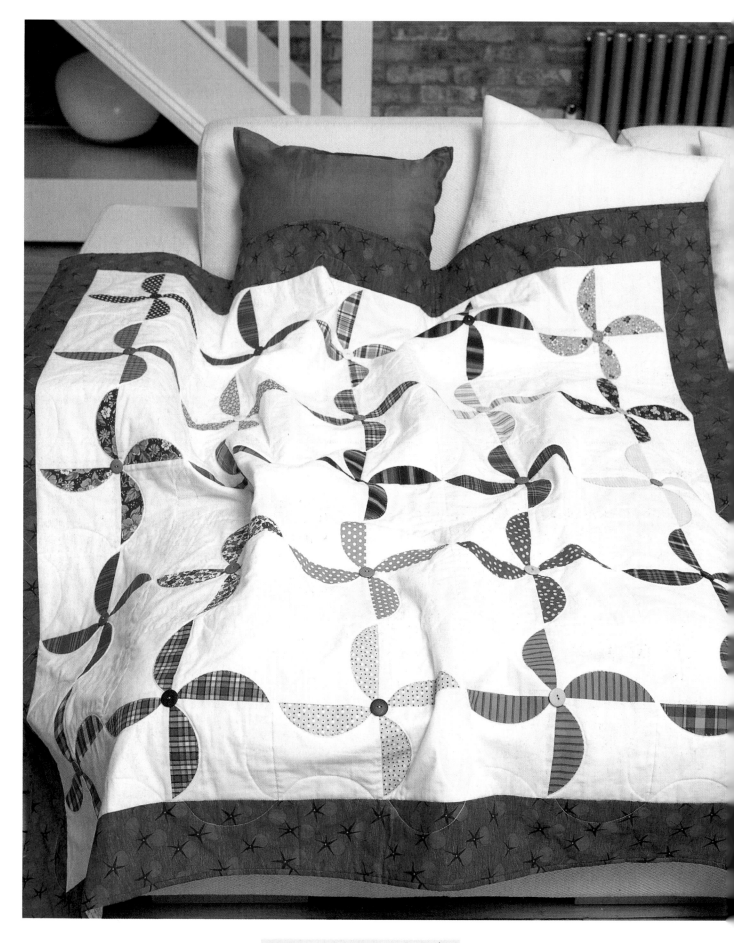

Appliqué Pinwheels

DESIGNED BY

Mary O'Riordan and Carol O'Riordan

This is a great beginner's project. The appliqué is simply a matter of tracing, pressing and cutting on the curves, and the piecing couldn't be easier. Bright checks and fresh floral prints always look crisp on a calico background, and the coloured buttons add a whimsical touch.

MATERIALS

All fabrics used in the quilt top are 45 in/115 cm wide, 100% cotton

Background fabric: white calico, 3 yds/2.75 m

Pinwheels: bright prints and checks, 1¼ yds/ 1.2 m in total. I have used a different fabric for each pinwheel – 25 in all (minimum amount required, 8 in/20 cm square) but you could use more of fewer fabrics and repeat the pinwheel colours.

Fusible webbing: 3½ yds/3.25 m, 15 in/38 cm wide

Template plastic

Borders and binding: blue fabric, 1¼ yds/1.2 m

Backing: 4 yds/3.75 m or a piece 68 in/170 cm square

Wadding: lightweight, 68 in/170 cm square

25 buttons

CUTTING

1 From the background fabric, cut 16 strips, 6 in/15 cm deep, across the width, then cross-cut into 100 x 6 in/15 cm squares.

2 Trace the pinwheel blade template on page 101 onto template plastic. Cut out as accurately as possible. Use the plastic template to trace 100 pinwheel blades on to the smooth side of the fusible web. Cut out the shapes just outside the marked lines (diagram 1).

diagram 1

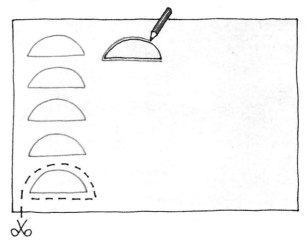

3 Press the fusible web shapes to the wrong side of the bright print and check fabrics. You need four of the same colour to make one pinwheel.

Quilt plan

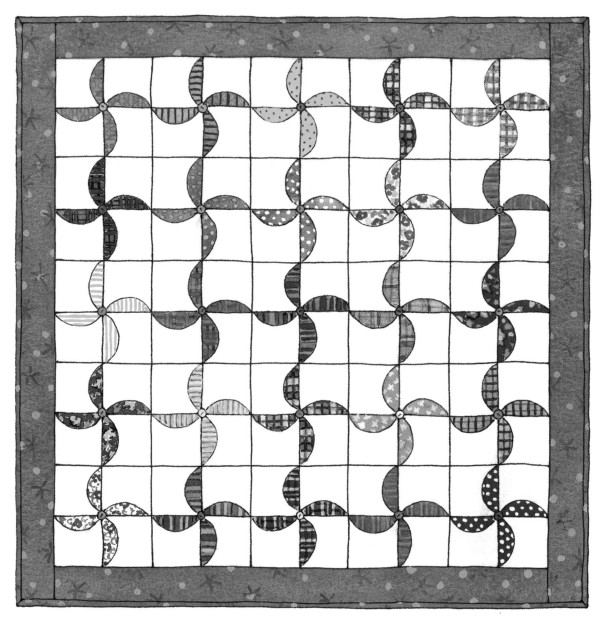

Finished size: $63\frac{1}{2}$ x $63\frac{1}{2}$ in/156 x 156 cm

TEMPLATE full size

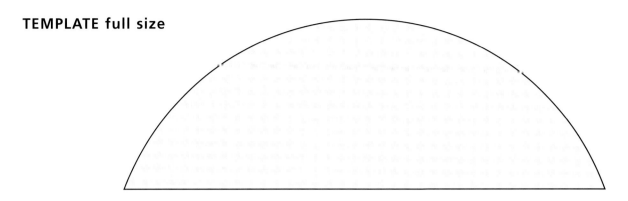

4 Cut out the pinwheel blades following accurately the marked lines on the fusible web papers.

5 From the blue fabric, cut six strips, 4½ in/12 cm deep, across the width for the borders; cut six strips, 2 in/5 cm deep, for the binding.

STITCHING

1 Remove the papers from the back of the fabrics and position one pinwheel blade, right side up, on each background square (diagram 2). Press to fuse in place. Zig-zag stitch along the curved edge of each blade.

diagram 2

2 Stitch four squares together, taking a ¼ in/0.75 cm seam allowance to make a block (diagram 3). Make 25 blocks.

diagram 3

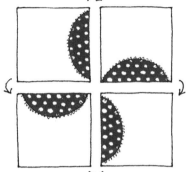

3 Following the quilt plan on page 100, pin and stitch the blocks into five rows of five blocks, taking the usual seam allowance. Pin and stitch the rows together, matching seams carefully, to complete the quilt top.

ADDING THE BORDERS

1 Stitch three of the blue 4½ in/12 cm wide border strips together. Measure the pieced top through the centre from side to side, then cut two strips to this measurement. Pin and stitch to the top and bottom of the quilt.

2 Stitch the remaining three blue 4½ in/12 cm wide border strips together. Measure the pieced top through the centre from top to bottom, then cut two strips to this measurement. Pin and stitch to the sides.

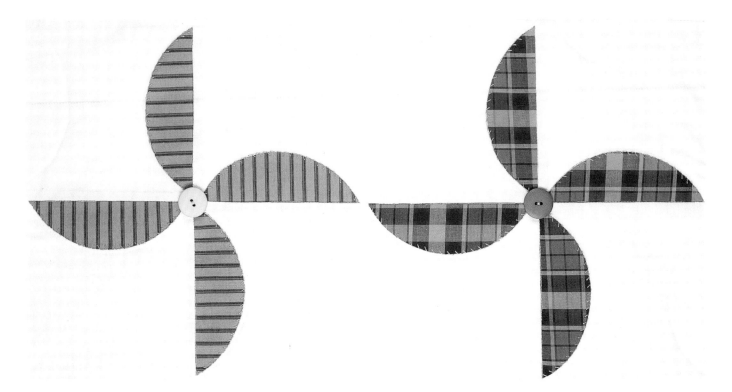

diagram 4

FINISHING

1 Spread the backing right side down on a flat surface, then smooth out the wadding and the pieced top, right side up, on top. Fasten together with safety pins or baste in a grid.

2 Beginning at the edge of the pieced block, machine or hand quilt in a continuous line, following the curves of the pinwheel blades all the way to the opposite edge. Rotate the quilt and return to the starting point along the centre seams of the pieced blocks (diagram 4).

3 Use the plastic template to mark a pinwheel in the space where four blocks meet, and quilt.

4 Stitch the binding strips with diagonal seams to make a continuous length to fit all around the quilt and use to bind the edges with a double-fold binding, mitred at the corners.

5 Stitch a button at the centre of each block.

Alternative colour schemes

1 Striped fabrics will highlight a background fabric and by alternating the direction of the lines in each unit the block has even more movement. **2** As each pinwheel blade requires a 6 x 2 in/15 x 5 cm rectangle of fabric, this is a good way to use up small scraps. **3** Make a romantic two-colour quilt using a single favourite fabric for the pinwheels on a white or neutral background. **4** For a really vibrant quilt choose bold fabrics for the background and the pinwheel blades, and use a different pair of fabrics for each block.

Blue and White Flowers

DESIGNED BY

Liz Lynch

This very simple quilt is an ideal project for lovers of hand work as it has virtually no piecing. The main section is divided into squares with quilting lines. Stylized blue and green flowers are appliquéd onto half the squares, while the remaining squares are quilted with a design that echoes the flowers. The quilting has been done by hand, although the straight lines could be machine quilted if desired.

MATERIALS

All fabrics used in the quilt top are 45 in/115 cm wide, 100% cotton

Background fabric: white, 1 yd/1 m

Borders and flower heads: pale blue floral, 24 in/60 cm

Corner blocks and flower heads: dark blue floral, fat quarter (18 x 22 in/ 50 x 56 cm)

Flower leaves and stems: green, fat quarter (18 x 22 in/50 x 56 cm)

Backing: 1½ yds/1.3 m

Wadding: lightweight, one piece 45 x 52 in/114 x 131 cm

Binding: blue, 18 in/40 cm

Template plastic

Template card or one packet of 1 in/ 2.5 cm, six-point diamond paper pieces. (Quilt top requires 75 pieces.)

CUTTING

1 From the background fabric, cut one piece across the width 34 in/87 cm deep. This will be cut down to size after the flowers have been applied.

2 From the pale blue fabric, cut two strips, 4½ x 33 in/11.5 x 84 cm, and two strips, 4½ x 39½ in/11.5 x 101.5 cm, for the borders. Reserve the remainder for the flower petals.

3 From the dark blue fabric, cut four 4½ in/11.5 cm corner squares. Reserve the remainder for the flower petals.

TEMPLATES full size

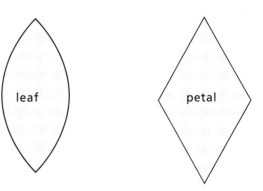

leaf

petal

Quilt plan

Finished size: 41 x 48 in/104 x 121 cm

diagram 1

4 From the blue fabric, cut four strips, 2½ in/
6 cm deep, across the width, for the binding.

5 From the green fabric, cut across the diagonal
at the longest point, three strips, 1 in/2.5 cm
wide, for the flower stems (diagram 1).
Reserve the remainder for the leaves.

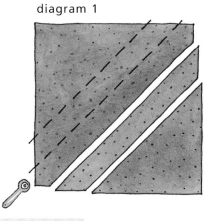

6 To create the flowers and the leaves, use templates A and B on page 105 to trace the leaf and petal shapes on to the template plastic. Cut out as accurately as possible, then use to make 75 paper diamond templates and 15 paper leaf templates.

7 Using the plastic template, trace 45 diamonds on to the light blue floral fabric, adding a ¼ in/0.75 cm allowance all round. Cut out on the marked seam allowance. Likewise, trace and cut 30 diamonds from the dark blue floral fabric. Cover the 75 paper templates with the fabric diamonds and baste to secure (diagram 2).

diagram 2

8 Use template A to cut 15 leaves from the green floral fabric, adding a ¼ in/0.75 cm allowance around each shape. Cover the paper leaf shapes with the fabric, and baste to secure (diagram 3).

diagram 3

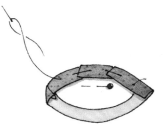

9 To make the stems, press each of the three 1 in/2.5 cm green strips in half lengthways, wrong sides together. Cross-cut the strips to provide 15 stems, each 4 in/10 cm long.

STITCHING

1 Following the quilt plan opposite, prepare the quilt top by lightly marking the background fabric with the marking pencil in a grid of 6½ in/16.5 cm squares, five squares across and six down. These will be the final quilting lines. Centralize the grid, but note that any excess fabric around the edge of the grid can be trimmed away later.

2 Start by applying a stem to the first square. Position the stem in a curve, leaving enough room for the flower to fit nicely into the block and with the folded edge of the stem on the outer curve (diagram 4).

diagram 4

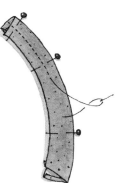

3 Pin and stitch down the centre of the stem with a fine backstitch in matching green thread. At the base of the stem turn up a small seam allowance and stitch down. Trim away the seam allowance close to the backstitch line, fold the stem over, and appliqué stitch along the folded edge. Do not push the fabric over too firmly, but allow a little leeway to give the stem dimension.

4 To make the flower heads, stitch five diamond shapes together using two dark and three pale blue fabrics (diagrams 5 and 6). Position with the template papers still in place, making sure to cover the raw top end of the stem. Pin and stitch using matching blue thread and appliqué stitch. Finally position the leaves as desired and stitch in place.

diagram 5   diagram 6

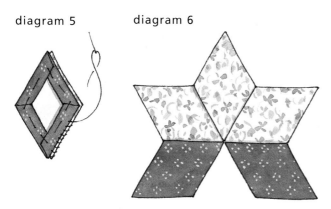

5 Remove all tacking threads. From the back of the work carefully cut away the background fabric to leave a ¼ in/0.75 cm seam and remove the template papers (diagram 7). The papers can be stored for future use.

diagram 7

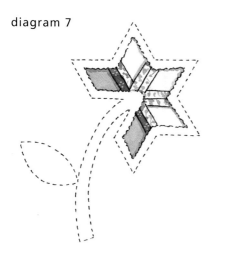

6 Place a 6½ in/16.5 cm square of template plastic on top of the appliquéd flower and with a dark pen, mark an outline of the flower, leaf and stem. Cut out. Use this as a template for the remaining blank squares to ensure all subsequent flowers are positioned exactly as the first one.

7 Repeat the appliqué process in the remaining 14 blocks, alternating every other block (see quilt plan).

8 Use the plastic template to mark the flower design quilting lines in the blank blocks.

ADDING THE BORDERS

1 Trim the main central section, leaving a ¼ in/ 0.75 cm seam allowance all around outside the central grid.

2 Pin and stitch the two short border strips to the top and bottom edges of the central section, taking the usual seam allowance. Press towards the borders.

3 Pin and stitch one dark blue corner square to one long border strip, right sides together and taking the usual seam allowance. Press towards the square. Repeat on the other end. Pin and stitch to one long side, taking the usual seam allowance. Press towards the border. Repeat to add the remaining border strip to the other long side.

FINISHING

1 Spread the backing right side down on a flat surface, then smooth out the wadding and the pieced top, right side up, on top. Fasten together with safety pins or baste in a grid.

2 Hand quilt the appliquéd flowers closely around their outline, and quilt the replicated flower design in the blank squares. Machine or hand quilt the grid lines.

3 Stitch the binding strips with diagonal seams to make a continuous length to fit all around the quilt and use to bind the edges with a double-fold binding, mitred at the corners.

Alternative colour schemes

1 The design relies on good contrast between the flowers and the background for maximum effect. Pink flowers would make a perfect quilt for a baby girl. **2** and **3** Primary colours give a striking, contemporary look for the toddler stage. **4** A striped background and white flowers take the quilt out of the nursery to create a lap quilt or table top that would look lovely in any room, especially at Christmas.

THE CONTRIBUTORS

Jane Coombes is a patchwork and quilting tutor and is a member of the teaching team at Creative Quilting near Hampton Court in Surrey.

Nikki Foley has a HNC in interior design and uses this to her advantage when designing quilts and patterns for her business 'The Sewing Shed': www.thesewingshed@aol.com

Janet Goddard writes patterns for magazines and books and teaches patchwork across Hertfordshire, Essex and North London.

Liz Lynch teaches classes in patchwork quilting at her studio near Truro, Cornwall and also at The Quilt Room in Dorking, Surrey.

Mary O'Riordan is an experienced quiltmaker who works at The Quilt Room in Dorking, Surrey

Gail Smith opened her shop, "Abigail Crafts", after completing a City and Guild course; she is a qualified adult education teacher, running local patchwork groups.

Sarah Wellfair is a qualified teacher who runs a full programme of workshops from her patchwork shop, Goose Chase Quilting, at Leckhampton in Gloucestershire.

Alison Wood teaches classes and works part-time at The Quilt Room in Dorking, Surrey.

Dorothy Wood is an author and designer who has written and contributed to over 20 needlecraft books.

SUPPLIERS

UK

Abigail Crafts
3-5 Regent Street
Stonehouse
Gloucestershire GL10 2AA
Tel: 01453 823691
www.abigailcrafts.co.uk
Patchwork and embroidery
supplies

The Bramble Patch
West Street
Weedon
Northants NN7 4QU
Tel: 01327 342212
Patchwork and quilting
supplies

Custom Quilting Limited
"Beal na Tra"
Derrymihan West
Castletownbere
Co Cork, Eire
Email: patches@iol.ie
Long arm quilting services

The Cotton Patch
1285 Stratford Road
Hall Green
Birmingham B28 9AJ
Tel: 0121 702 2840
Patchwork and quilting
supplies

Creative Quilting
3 Bridge Road
East Molesey
Surrey KT8 9EU
Tel: 020 8941 7075
Specialist retailer

Fred Aldous Ltd
P.O Box 135
37 Lever Street
Manchester M1 1LW
Tel: 0161 236 2477
Mail order craft materials

Goose Chase Quilting
65 Great Norwood Street
Leckhampton
Cheltenham GL50 2BQ
Tel: 01242 512639
Patchwork and quilting
supplies

Hab-bits
Unit 9, Vale Business Park
Cowbridge
Vale of Glamorgan
CF71 7PF
Tel: 01446 775150
Haberdashery supplies

Patchwork Direct
c/o Heirs & Graces
King Street
Bakewell
Derbyshire DE45 1DZ
Tel: 01629 815873
www.patchworkdirect.com
Patchwork and quilting
supplies

Purely Patchwork
23 High Street
Linlithgow
West Lothian
Scotland
Tel: 01506 846200
Patchwork and quilting
supplies

The Quilt Loft
9/10 Havercroft Buildings
North Street
Worthing
West Sussex BN11 1DY
Tel: 01903 233771
Quilt supplies, classes and
workshops

The Quilt Room
20 West Street
Dorking
Surrey RH4 1BL
Tel: 01306 740739
www.quiltroom.co.uk
Quilt supplies, classes and
workshops
Mail order: The Quilt Room
c/o Carvilles
Station Road
Dorking
Surrey RH4 1XH
Tel: 01306 877307

Quilting Solutions
Firethorn
Rattlesden Road
Drinkstone
Bury St Edmunds
Suffolk IP30 9TL
Tel: 01449 735280
Email:
firethorn@lineone.net
www.quiltingsolutions.co.uk
Long arm quilting services

The Sewing Shed
Shanahill West
Keel
Castlemaine
Co Kerry, Eire
Tel: 00 35366 9766931
www.thesewingshed@eir-com.net
Patchwork and quilting
supplies

SUPPLIERS

Stitch in Time
293 Sandycombe Road
Kew
Surrey TW9 3LL
Tel: 020 8948 8462
www.stitchintimeuk.com
Specialist quilting retailer

Strawberry Fayre
Chagford
Devon TQ13 8EN
Tel: 01647 433250
Mail order fabrics and quilts

Sunflower Fabrics
157-159 Castle Road
Bedford MK40 3RS
Tel: 01234 273819
www.sunflowerfabrics.com
Quilting supplies

Worn and Washed
The Walled Garden
48 East Street
Olney
Bucks MK 46 4DW
Tel: 01234 240881
Email:kim@wornand-
washedfabrics.com

South Africa

Crafty Supplies
Stadium on Main
Main Road
Claremont 7700
Tel: 021 671 0286
Fern Gully
46 3rd Street
Linden
2195
Tel: 011 782 7941

Stitch 'n' Stuff
140 Lansdowne Road
Claremont 7700
Tel: 021 674 4059

Pied Piper
69 1st Avenue
Newton Park
Port Elizabeth 6001
Tel: 041 365 1616

Quilt Talk
40 Victoria Street
George 6530
Tel: 044 873 2947

Nimble Fingers
Shop 222
Kloof Village Mall
Village Road
Kloof 3610
Tel: 031 764 6283

Quilt Tech
9 Louanna Avenue
Kloofendal
Extension 5 1709
Tel: 011 679 4386

Simply Stitches
2 Topaz Street
Albernarle
Germiston 1401
Tel: 011 902 6997

Quilting Supplies
42 Nellnapius Drive
Irene 0062
Tel: 012 667 2223

Australia

Country Patchwork Cottage
10/86 Erindale Road
Balcatta
WA 6021
Tel: (08) 9345 3550
The Quilters Store
22 Shaw Street
Auchenflower
QLD 4066
Tel: (07) 3870 0408

Patchwork of Essendon
96 Fletcher Street
Essendon
VIC 3040
Tel: (03) 9372 0793

Patchwork Plus
Shop 81
7-15 Jackson Avenue
Miranda
NSW 2228
Tel: (02) 9540 278

Quilts and Threads
827 Lower North East Road
Dernancourt
SA 5075
Tel: (08) 8365 6711

Riverlea Cottage Quilts
Shop 4, 330 Unley Road
Hyde Park
SA 5061
Tel: (08) 8373 0653

New Zealand

Grandmothers Garden
Patchwork and Quilting
1042 Gordonton Road
Gordonton
Hamilton
Tel: (07) 824 3050

**Hands Ashford Craft Supply
Store**
5 Normans Road
Christchurch
Tel: (03) 355 9099
www.hands.co.nz

Needlecraft Distributors
600 Main Street
Palmerston North
Tel: (06) 356 4793
Fax: (06) 355 4594

Patchwork Barn
132 Hinemoa Street
Birkenhead
Auckland
Tel: (09) 480 5401

The Patchwork Shop
356 Grey Street
Hamilton
Tel: (07) 856 6365

The Quilt Shop
35 Pearn Place
Northcote Shopping Centre
Auckland
Tel: (09) 480 0020
Fax: (09) 480 0380

Spotlight Stores
Whangarei (09) 430 7220
Wairau Park (09) 444 0220
Henderson (09) 836 0888
Panmure (09) 527 0915
Manukau City (09) 263 6760
Hamilton (07) 839 1793
Rotorua (07) 343 6901
New Plymouth (06) 757 3575
Gisborne (06) 863 0037
Hastings (06) 878 5223
Palmerston North (06) 357
6833
Porirua (04) 238 4055
Wellington (04) 472 5600
Christchurch (03) 377 6121
Dunedin (03) 477 1478
www.spotlight.net.nz

Stitch and Craft
32 East Tamaki Road
Papatoetoe
Auckland
Tel: (09) 278 1351
Fax: (09) 278 1356

Stitches
351 Colombo Street
Christchurch
Tel: (03) 379 1868
Fax: (03) 377 2347
www.stitches.co.nz

Variety Handcrafts
106 Princes Street
Dunedin
Tel: (03) 474 1088

INDEX